CRUCIBLE

"A container of metal or refractory material
employed for heating substances to high temperatures;
a severe, searching test or trial."

Random House Dictionary of the English Lanaguage,
Second Edition Unabridged, 1966, Random House N.Y., N.Y.

Just as the intense heat of a crucible melts metals within it,
so the privation, suffering and stress
of arrest, imprisonment and rescue in war
tests the courage, faith and stamina of all who survive it.

We Survived War's Crucible

*A True Story of Imprisonment and
Rescue in World War II Philippines*

*The Autobiographical Wartime Experiences of
Stephen Lloyd Smith, Viola and their son, Paul.*

EDITED AND WRITTEN BY
DONALD P. SMITH

authorHOUSE®

AuthorHouse™
1663 Liberty Drive, Suite 200
Bloomington, IN 47403
www.authorhouse.com
Phone: 1-800-839-8640

This book is a work of non-fiction. Unless otherwise noted, the author and the publisher make no explicit guarantees as to the accuracy of the information contained in this book and in some cases, names of people and places have been altered to protect their privacy.

First published by AuthorHouse 12/18/2007

ISBN: 978-1-4343-2968-4 (e)
ISBN: 978-1-4343-2967-7 (sc)

Library of Congress Control Number: 2007907128

Printed in the United States of America
Bloomington, Indiana

This book is printed on acid-free paper.

Cover design by Jeffrey Smith

Contents

Preface   vii

Chapter One   Caught in the Crucible   1

Chapter Two   Love in the Crucible   15

Chapter Three   Life in the Crucible   23

Chapter Four   The Crucible Heats Up   34

Chapter Five   Overwhelming Pressure Intensifies   41

Chapter Six   Rescue   54

Chapter Seven   Out of the Rubble and into Eternity   69

Addendum   My First Career in Isolated Rural Philippines   77

Bibliography   89

About the Author   90

Stephen L. Smith, the subject of this book, would never have taken time to write about himself and his experiences. He was too absorbed in the lives of others, in preaching and teaching, and in carrying on his ministry of love and compassion for those whose lives touched his.

Yet most of this war time story is in the words of the subject himself, recorded in one way or another prior to his death. Dad was a consummate story teller and he did share his experiences with others. After his retirement from the Philippines while serving as Assistant Pastor of the First Presbyterian Church of Watsonville, California, he was persuaded to tell his life story in an organized way to the Adult Bible Class in that congregation. His grandson, Stephen Randall Smith recorded those sessions. In addition I interviewed him at length over a two or three year period, and recorded the interviews on tape. These tapes were laboriously transcribed and edited.

He left a written record of many of his experiences in his annual reports submitted to the Board of Foreign Missions of the Presbyterian Church in the U.S.A. and in a number of articles he wrote for <u>The Philippine Presbyterian</u>, a periodical published for many years by the Philippine Presbyterian Mission. In dealing with this printed material I have incorporated long passages of narrative without using quotation marks, since the text was written by my father. Sometimes I felt it necessary to edit those inserts.

To this material I have added descriptive passages from my own recollections whenever I felt it would help the reader visualize unfamiliar places, objects or situations, or to clarify an important theme. As editor of the extensive transcriptions from the tapes, I have sometimes modified awkward oral communication to use more felicitous written language or to make a smooth transition from one topic to another.

In order to maintain the flow of the narrative, I have felt free, in a few cases, to put material secured from my mother, Viola Rich Smith, or other members of the family, into the first person singular, as though they were my father's own words. More extensively, I have done this in sections which were immeasurably enriched by stories told by my late brother Paul Lincoln Smith, who shared in the war time trials described here. He remembered many interesting incidents and added important details to the narrative. In almost every instance, when Paul is mentioned, the source was Paul himself. About a year before he died, I recorded his experiences on tape and have used his transcribed stories liberally throughout the book. He had reviewed early drafts of those chapters and knew I was going to use his stories here. Including them is a fitting tribute to him. I feel confident he would have agreed to the treatment I have used.

In making these changes, I have served as both editor and author. In all, I have sought faithfully to represent the spirit and style of my father whom I can best describe as a modern saint. However, I take full responsibility for what is written here, since it was not possible for him to read this account and correct any inaccuracies that may have crept into it. Dad made an indelible impression on my life, and on the lives of countless others. I felt compelled to write his biography. I have shared it with members of our family and others who knew and loved him. This book contains chapters of that biography which describe our family's wartime experiences. I trust that those who read will find it a fascinating and uplifting experience of God's hand in the crucible of war. In unpublished parts of that biography I was able to record stories of his life before the war. The Addendum following chapter seven contains some of his more interesting early experiences in the mountains and rivers of Southern Luzon and on neighboring islands.

Having been born in Legaspi, Albay and lived there until I was 17, I remember many things about those early years which have no room in a book such as this, but which give me a perspective that has been invaluable in organizing this story. I borrowed some of Otho LaPorte's adjectives in describing the spectacular eruptions of Mayon volcano. Having lived in Manila, with my wife Verna, for five years after the war, I can picture the settings of the wartime years and have tried to convey them faithfully.

I am indebted to the staff of the Department of History of the Presbyterian Church (U.S.A.) in Philadelphia for making available the documents which have been essential to this task. Thanks also are due the Global Mission Ministry Unit of the same Church for permission to use material from <u>The Philippine Presbyterian</u> and from my father's and mother's annual reports.

Toward the end of my initial work on this book, my conversations with Paul and Jean Dotson and with Kyoji Buma led my wife and me to a personal contact with Johnny Fujita, whose wartime experiences are described in chapter two. Meeting him and his lovely wife was one of the delights of my research.

As the book was being designed, it was a great joy to be able to ask our grandson, Jeffrey Smith, a graphic artist, to design the front cover. My gratitude to him for a superb job!

Finally, I am indebted beyond words, to my loving wife Verna, without whose patience and understanding, during the many hours I have spent in front of my computer, this book would never have been completed. She reviewed the manuscript, helped in the copyediting and made many helpful suggestions which have significantly improved the work.

DONALD P. SMITH
Pompton Plains, New Jersey
September 25, 2007

CHAPTER ONE

CAUGHT IN THE CRUCIBLE

Two days after Pearl Harbor the Japanese were bombing both ships and shore in Manila Bay and I had to get back to Manila. I was an unexpected passenger on a Coast Guard Cutter just outside the bay. My passport to that ship had been three stranded American soldiers who needed to get back to their units in Manila.

We entered Manila Bay exactly at the time the Japanese were bombing the Naval communication center at Cavite, just outside Manila. They had hit two of the three radio towers and demolished them. Only one of them was still standing.

We went through the mine fields between Corregidor and the mainland. I was glad it was a Coast Guard Cutter, and hoped they knew where the mines were. At least they had some idea what the situation was. We got through all right.

Just after we cleared the mine fields the Japanese bombers flew right over us. The anti-aircraft guns of Corregidor tried to reach them but those guns weren't adequate at all. And the big guns on the island couldn't do any good either. They were all aimed out to sea. There wasn't anything our defenses could do. The Japanese planes were much too high and they just flew over. I stood there looking up, watching the antiaircraft shells bursting way below them. The incapacity of those air raid guns on Corregidor was obvious. Suddenly some shrapnel fell in the water near us. Quickly I pulled in my head.

As we got into Manila, we saw five or six ships sunk in the bay from that bombing, and some were burning.

Those three American officers, who had never had any combat duty, were as terrified as I was. They were taking brandy to get up their

1

courage, and couldn't understand why I didn't take some. By the time we got in, they were pretty well tacked on booze. They were too happy to know what was happening. It was a frightening trip.

We landed at Legaspi Landing at the Luneta. I don't know where the others went. There I was, alone with my two suitcases, the brief case and the typewriter. The air raid was on and there was no public transportation. We lived about two miles away in Malate. So I grabbed the brief case and the typewriter, left the suitcases there, and walked home. Nothing was moving. I got our car out and drove back. The air raid was still on. The suitcases were still there! They were untouched! Nobody was going anywhere. Everybody was afraid, and stayed under shelter. I just defied the air raid.

But where were Viola and Paul?

In 1940, almost a year before Pearl Harbor, I arrived in Manila with my wife, Viola, and our16 year-old son, Paul. The Presbyterian Board of Foreign Missions had appointed me as Executive Secretary and Acting Treasurer of their Philippine Mission.

In the weeks before the war things were quite unsettled. The air was filled with news of war and rumors of war. Paul had worked his way into a job as announcer on a couple of Manila's radio stations. The station car would pick him up in the wee small hours of the morning and he would sign on KZRF at 6:00 a.m. and KZRM at 6:30. At 7:00 he would ride his bicycle to high school, and would be back on the air in the evening to sign off the stations at night. In fact, I believe his was the last voice on the air when Manila fell.

Paul was involved in news broadcasting. Once a week the staff did a weekly dramatization of the news. He greatly enjoyed the challenge of creating wartime sound effects when they were dramatizing Hitler's invasion into some country.

On one program they had to have some tanks, and their sound effect records had no tanks on them. So, they took metal folding chairs lying

2

flat in two stacks next to each other. Two persons alternately would reach down into a stack and pick up the upper back part of the chairs, lift them off the floor just a little bit, and let them trickle through their fingers. When one was getting near the end of his stack, the other would pick up his stack and let them trickle through his fingers. Thus, they made a continuous tank sound live in the studio. Another challenge was to get the sound of a gunshot. They tried cap pistols. Nothing seemed to work. Finally Paul just hit a padded chair with a ruler and, on microphone, it sounded like a gunshot.

War was constantly in the news. Then came the blackouts. Things began to look ominous. The possibility of an attack existed and the authorities wanted to be ready. Blackouts in prewar Manila were taken quite seriously. After a few trial runs they notified everybody that if lights did not go out on future blackouts they would be shot out. After a sharpshooter shot out some lights, people soon realized that the authorities really did mean business and the lights would go out when the siren sounded.

There was a general feeling that anything might happen. One of our missionary families was so jittery that, as Executive Secretary, I finally decided I had to send them home immediately, without referring the decision to the headquarters in New York. I got a little slap on the wrist for doing it, but it was a situation that had to be handled. I couldn't wait for Board action. It had to be done right then!

I was acting treasurer until a week before Pearl Harbor when Alexander Christie came out to take over that office. I was still Executive Secretary of the Mission.

Our Silliman University, on a southern island, was building a church. The province of Oriental Negros had started building a pier in Dumaguete, where Silliman was located, and was unable to complete it. They had on hand steel and cement and other things they were willing to sell us. It was difficult to get building material and Silliman wanted permission to buy it. So I went to Dumaguete, several hundred miles south of Manila, to look it over and authorize its purchase. I went by steamship on a round trip ticket.

3

Because of the International Date Line, December 7, 1941 was Monday, December 8 in the Philippines. When we heard about Pearl Harbor, we had a rather exciting time at the University deciding what we were going to do. Silliman got busy working out their war strategy, and set up an emergency organization, with Roy Bell as captain of safety arrangements.

Suddenly all transportation was cut off. The boat I had taken became a troop ship. Here I was in Dumaguete in the southern part of the Philippines. Viola and Paul were in Manila. I was determined to get back to Manila, to my family and to all my important responsibilities.

As soon as our meetings were over, I got one of the professors to take me in his car up to the northern part of the island. We went to a place where there usually was a seagoing ferry across to the next island of Cebu. We didn't know whether there would be any ferry there at all, but at least he would take me there and I hoped I could get one. There was no other transportation. No air transportation, and the steamship line was no longer carrying passengers, because of the war.

Fortunately the regular ferry was waiting there. I took my two suitcases, a brief case and a typewriter and put them aboard. My friend left me, and that was it! From there on I was going to do whatever opened up. What I would find on the other side, I didn't know. Where would I go from there? The bus I was hoping to get at the tip of Cebu Island would go along a narrow mountain road to Cebu City, in the middle of the island, about four or five hours away. In the city of Cebu there might be transportation. I took every step of this way as a venture of faith.

Eventually, we crossed to Cebu island. When we got to the other side, in the late afternoon, the bus was there waiting. I got on board with my baggage. We waited and waited. Finally we took off. Night fell. With the war situation as it was, they couldn't use their headlights. They were afraid there might be a bombing raid in the night. So they put carbon paper over the headlights and made a little hole that would let a little light out. The bus, with very dim blue headlights, made its way along this narrow mountain road. To go up over the mountains with hooded headlights was a rather frightening experience!

As we traveled, I wondered. When we did get to Cebu what would I find there? Where would they land us? What next, I didn't know. Where would I go from there? We got into Cebu city about 1:00 a.m. At that time of night how would I get across the city with all my baggage? It happened that three or four other passengers on that bus wanted a taxi, and there was one there. We got aboard, put our baggage on our laps and the driver took us over to the wharf.

There at the pier was the Panay, the ship I had gone down on. It had become a troop ship and was full of raw recruits, Filipinos with very little if any training, barefoot, some of them with very poor uniforms. They had not been outfitted yet. They were on their way to be trained and outfitted. I had a return ticket on that boat, so without asking any questions I just carried my baggage aboard, stowed it near a chair and sat down. I had no cabin, of course.

Where my ship was going, I didn't know. But I realized, I had better try to get a message through to Viola. So I went across to the Post Office. It was closed, but the telegraph office on the second floor was operating. They had blackout curtains. I persuaded them to accept a telegram. But they said, "We can't guarantee it will get through." The telegram did reach her all right, but she didn't know what to do. The message couldn't give her anything definite because I didn't know anything except that I was trying to get to Manila.

Meanwhile, back in Manila the bombing had begun in earnest. At first the raids were all at night. Within hours after Pearl Harbor, Clark Field was hit and then bombs fell on Nichols Field and the Cavite Naval base, near Manila. There was some bombing down by the Luneta near the Walled City, where there must have been some anti-aircraft gun emplacements. But, I knew nothing of all that in Cebu at the time.

We didn't sail from Cebu until about seven or eight the next morning. About breakfast time a cabin boy came to me asking, "Are you a German?" I replied, "No, I'm an American." Well, he said, "There are three American soldiers at the table over there. They'd like to have you join them." I went over and had breakfast with them. They were eager to get back to their command.

While we were at breakfast, we heard telegraph dots and dashes that I couldn't understand at all. Fortunately one of these men was a communications officer. He recognized that it was Spanish, not English. "I think the Captain is asking for directions," he said. "We'd better go up and talk to him." The three of them rushed up to the bridge to talk to the Captain and find out where he was going. I didn't go. They had more clout than I would have, so I just sat there and waited. The Captain said, "We are not sure whether we are going on to Manila or not. But we might. We'll try to take care of you." Of course it was very important for these officers to connect with their command. During the day we watched some of the recruits practice shooting at kite targets off the ship, and stumbling over each other.

Finally, it was Wednesday morning. I had been traveling one whole day and two nights. We were off the Batangas coast and nearing Manila. The captain was still waiting for instructions. Was he to try getting to Manila or not? So he said, "Now there is a Coast Guard cutter just ahead. We'll overtake it before long and we'll transfer you to that cutter if you want. I know it's going to Manila." The officers agreed to be transferred at sea, and invited me to join them. I said, "Yes, I'll go along with you." They loaded us into a lifeboat and took us over to the Coast Guard cutter. That's how I got back to Manila.

By the time I returned to the house with the luggage, Viola had come back. She had received my telegram the day before I arrived. So she went down to the Maritima Lines' office and tried to find out when my ship would come in. The shipping executive said, "I can't tell you anything. But, you go to the wharf tomorrow morning."

The next day she was on her way to the wharf, when all of a sudden the sirens sounded and the planes were already right over them. The police drove everyone into the basement of the Heacock Building. That's where she was when the raid was on. As soon as she could, she went up to the top of the Heacock Building and over to the fire escape. Out in the bay ships were burning and huge clouds of black smoke arose from Corregidor. Fort Stotsenburg was burning. She knew I was supposed to be on a ship coming into the bay. She watched with fear and trembling. Then she just had to go down and get home.

Viola came out of the Heacock Building onto the Escolta, one of the main shopping streets of the city. There wasn't a soul there! Not a rig! Not an automobile! And, not a person! Finally a man came along in his small car and asked, "Madam, where are you going? Where do you live?" "I live in Malate," she replied. "Get in," he said. "I'm the manager of the Jai Alai and I'll take you that far." He took her there and she walked the rest of the way home.

"As I walked home," she recalled, "the trucks, like covered wagons, were coming in with the injured and taking them to the hospital on the banks of the Pasig river. That was one of the terrible times, trying to get home through all of this. Walking alone. It was quite a distance, a little over half way down town. I was never more relieved and joyous to see Stephen than when he walked in that door. I didn't know whether we would ever see each other again."

As soon as Viola got home, she turned on the radio to get Paul's station. He was supposed to be on duty there, and the Japanese had been trying to bomb the radio stations. So she wanted to hear his station on the air. It was.

Since Pearl Harbor, Paul had been living at the radio studios. There was a curfew from seven at night to seven in the morning. Someone had to stay at the radio station to sign off at night, carry on radio warfare jamming with Tokyo, and then sign on the next morning; all between curfews. Our son Paul fell into that almost automatically. All the commercial programs were off the air. The stations were in close touch with the Army at all times. The army laid out the schedule related to sign off and sign on times. The station's staff was decimated. Many were on assignment with the U.S. Army.

Both stations ran one set of programs rather than the usual two. Paul would sign on at six in the morning. His first relief came in about nine o'clock. Paul Eldridge, a Seventh Day Adventist preacher, who had been doing a half hour devotional once a week, had volunteered to do a daily half hour devotional during this time. That gave Paul a chance to go downstairs and get some breakfast. Then he would come back at 9:30 and make sure there was somebody else there or he would go back on the air himself. Other station staff would come as they could, but Paul was the main continuity for the announcing on the two stations. At curfew time in the evening, Paul would be back on the air again, and everybody else would be gone, except for one engineer who stayed with Paul at the station. And of course there were engineers out at the transmitter. At ten, Paul would give a final news broadcast and sign off. Then Paul and the engineer would take a break and get set up for radio warfare with Tokyo.

Japan's big propaganda broadcast of the evening came on shortwave at eleven p.m. On one turntable Paul would put the loudest march he could locate. And on the other turntable he would put the hottest piece of jazz he could find. Then he would feed them both down the line together. Every once in a while he would open the mike and howl and then turn it off for a bit. Meantime, in the control room on the other side of the glass, Tuason, the engineer, would be picking up the whole mess, mixing it with Tokyo's broadcast and with the other two commercial stations in Manila that were also jamming Tokyo.

Out at the transmitters the engineers would move their frequency as close to Tokyo as possible, broadcast all that noise, and try to blanket them on both sides. But Tokyo was set up for that sort of thing. They could easily move their frequency at will. So the engineers in the Manila sation transmitters really had to work. Their transmitters were not designed for varying their frequencies. It was quite a job for them to follow the changes that Tokyo would make. Of course, Tokyo had such a powerful signal, that if anyone really wanted to listen to them and were willing to follow them, they could, but it wasn't easy listening.

When Paul and Tuason finished jamming, they quit and went to sleep. Then they got up again at 5:30 and got ready to sign on at six. That was Paul's day. Once in a while when there was a long enough break and somebody else was on the air, Paul would hop on his bicycle and come home in the daytime for a visit.

The first daylight bombing was the morning when I arrived from Cebu. That day Paul had gotten some relief and went home for lunch. He was on his bicycle going back to the radio station when the bombing began. Planes were way up there and the bombs were falling. Paul jumped off his bicycle and took it into a little clump of trees on the front lawn of the Philippine General Hospital. He dropped the bicycle to the ground and was lying down with it. Suddenly he remembered stories of the bombing of hospitals in China. "Boy," he said to himself, "If they do the same thing here, this is not the place to be hanging out." So, quickly he jumped on the bike and started heading for the radio station again. A National Defense volunteer guard was stopping all traffic. Everybody had to pull over.

Paul had put a little sign on the front of his bicycle that said KZRM. He had taken it off the ring stand at the station when some equipment was being discarded. So whenever Paul was stopped, he would point to the KZRM on the front of his bicycle and the guard would wave him through. About every two blocks Paul would run through that same routine again and get waved through.

When he got down to the Post Office, he had to negotiate a long curving ramp and go over the Quezon Bridge into the Quiapo area in order to reach his studios. "Never in my life," Paul told us, "have I ever pedaled a bicycle any harder than when I crossed that bridge. I never knew when that bridge might become a target, and I sure didn't want to be there when it did." But he got to work, locked up his bicycle, and went upstairs to an area they used for shelter.

By the grace of God, all three of us finally got together. I will never forget that trip from Dumaguete to Manila. I didn't know how safe I would be if I had stayed in Dumaguete. But I had to get back to Manila. And I'm glad I did because I was needed there. I didn't know what the future would be. But it turned out that it was important for me to take care of our missionary community.

There was air raid after air raid. We would no sooner get dinner on the table than an air raid would come. We would rush across the street to the high school. It was a concrete building, and part of the partitions were concrete. We had a shelter under the concrete stairs. And there were sand bags in front of the doors of the classrooms opposite the stairs. Under that cement stairway was about as safe a place as we could find. So, we would go there whenever there was an air raid. But, sometimes a raid would come on so fast that the best we could do was to get under the bed.

Once when we were in the air raid shelter, a limousine pulled up in front of the High school. In it was Mrs. Douglas McArthur, their boy, and their amah. I went out to greet them and invited her to take shelter with us. But she said, "No, I'll just cruise around." They were living in a penthouse on top of the Manila Hotel, rather a conspicuous place for a bombing. She didn't want to stay up in their penthouse, and thought she would be safer just cruising around in a car. She didn't come in, but we had a little visit. That's where I got acquainted with her.

On Christmas eve the Japanese bombed Los Baños. They hit a water tank just 20 or 30 feet from the Mission house. Several families had gone from Manila out to Los Baños for safety. They had thought they would be better off there than in Manila. Some of us decided otherwise. We stayed in Manila. When that water tank was bombed, one of the missionaries, who had a car, came back to Manila with his family. He arranged for two of our cars to go with him back to Los Baños to bring the rest of the people.

We left about sunset. It was a good moonlit night, but clouds were gathering as we went up the slope from Cavite. To get to Los Baños, we had to go around a back road that none of us had ever been on before. The main road was being paved, a section here, and another section there. So it was a one way road into Manila. I think if we had known what we would have to go through, we would have ventured to go the wrong way, on that one way road. Besides, there wasn't a lot of traffic then. At any rate, we went the proper way, up the hill, over a road we didn't know. Three or four times Filipino sentries stopped us and challenged our passage.

We got to Los Baños near midnight, tired as could be. Some of our people were not there in the house. After the bombing, they had gone to some other houses. We couldn't gather them together right away. But there were enough folks there for one car load to go right back. So, I drove back and left the other two cars to wait for the remaining passengers. I preferred to go back at night than to risk the bombing in the daytime. Now, I was going back over the road I knew, because it was one way toward Manila. As we had been told to do, I had carbon paper over my headlights, with a little hole in it. That hole let enough light go through to keep from colliding with anybody, but not enough to give us any light on the road. I was crawling along that way, when a blue light from behind caught up with me. The man in that American Army vehicle asked, "Where are you going?" "To Manila," I replied. He looked at my headlights and blurted out, "Get that paper off those lights." I did. Then he said, "Now. There's a group of vehicles ahead. Catch up with them, and follow us in." I did.

We got into Manila about dawn. Just after dawn we were roughly five or six miles from home, and there was an air raid. We got out in a ditch and waited until that was over and then went on home. I have never been more tired in my life than when I got home that time.

Close to the end of December, when Paul was talking on the air, their transmitters in Bulacan were blown up as our retreating troops were leaving. So Paul may well have been the last announcer on the air in Manila, before the Japanese took over the city. When the radio went off the air, I picked Paul up in the car. He just left his bicycle and some personal things at the station and never went back. He could have used that bicycle during our house arrest period, but it was gone!

Fortunately, Paul's boss, Noel Araneta, was a very wise man. When he knew the Japanese were going to occupy Manila he burned all the personnel records at the station. So the invaders had no knowledge of who had been announcing. That probably saved Paul. Of course we have no way of telling whether Paul would have been "interrogated." As far as the invading army knew, when we were picked up, Paul was just a high school student, son of missionaries, period. Paul never mentioned that he had worked there. Later he saw one of the CBS correspondents in the Los Baños concentration camp. He was about to greet her. But when she saw Paul she made a quick shake of the head and ignored him completely. Paul got the message that they shouldn't give each other away. He made no contact with her.

Manila had been declared an open city. Our forces got out of the city and did not try to defend it. On January first, Japanese officers met with Filipino officials to arrange the take-over of the city. The victorious troops came into Manila on the second of January 1942. We sat on our porch and watched their parade go by on Taft Avenue. We didn't know just what they would do, but we had talked it over and decided we would not go out into the country. We would rather deal with responsible officers than with underlings who might catch us out there. We decided to stay in Manila.

On January second and third they started picking up those they considered to be dangerous military or political prisoners. Then on the sixth of January they picked us up. Our house was on the northwest corner of Wright and Tennessee streets. Doctor and Mrs. Stevenson lived next door to us on Wright Street. The Buchers, a missionary family transplanted from Hainan, China lived behind us on Tennessee Street. One group of soldiers came toward our corner along Tennessee and another came toward us on Wright Street.

We were gathered outside our front door waiting. Viola came down the steps putting on her hat. She stuck a hat pin through it. Military vehicles pulled up in front of our houses on Wright Street. Before the soldiers got to us, Louise Bucher, over on Tennessee called out, "They've taken Henry and left me with the children." She was about eight months' pregnant. "What am I going to do?" she cried. "Here I have these children and they've taken Henry. What am I going to do?" The Japanese have a high regard for babies, for pregnant women and for old people. These are top priority categories in their culture. Furthermore, they didn't want any births in the camp. And if any wife became pregnant there they put her in a house of unwed mothers. They didn't want any births in the camp, so they left her there, alone in the house.

A soldier arrived for us. "You come," he said. Viola pulled her hat pin out of her hat as a way of saying that she planned to stay. She took off her hat, laid it down on the steps, and said, "Must stay!" The Japanese said, "Oh no! You come. You come!" But Viola said, "No, You come." And made him follow her on a path around a big tree to where Louise was standing at the fence between our houses. "Look at that," Viola said. "She needs help. We can't leave her there." It happened that this man could speak some English and was understanding. He nodded. "Ah . . . So . . . deska," he responded. "You stay. You stay!" So we got him to agree to let Viola stay to take care of Louise. He wrote up something that qualified her as a midwife.

On the basis of that, Viola stayed out. Then I said, "Now. There is a doctor next door, the other way. If you let him stay, then everything will be all right." They did. So, with Viola in the corner house, Louise next door on one side, and Dr. Stevenson on the other side, our three residences were kept safe until we got out of our brief initial internment. The baby wasn't born until after we came back.

All the rest of us were taken out in cars to Rizal Memorial Stadium. We took a few things with us. Out on the field we lined up. There were quite a few lines because enemy aliens were being picked up from all over the city and being processed there. At tables the Japanese officers checked our passports, and that sort of thing. After we went through that process, we were taken to Santo Tomas University on the North side of the Pasig River, which was being used as a concentration camp. Now, our family was split. Our son's Stephen and Donald were in California. Paul and I were interned in Santo Tomas, and Viola was at home in Manila.

Paul and I scrambled for some place to sleep. We got some desks and put them together, arranging them so that the lower side of each sloping desk met the lower side of another and we slept in the valley. But no matter how you arrange them, sloping desks don't exactly make the most comfortable bed. But we managed somehow.

Early the very next morning after our arrival, there were some Filipinos outside the fence, bringing stuff for the internees. And they were just giving them! Oh, they were wonderful! The Japanese didn't like our getting all that attention, so they soon put a stop to it.

Those who were interned were foreigners from countries that were hostile to Japan. Citizens of other countries were not interned. One very helpful woman, I think she was German, came to Viola and told her they were going to take us all to Taiwan. There was Viola, out of the camp and alone. And, for all she knew, I was going to Taiwan with Paul! Would she ever see us again?

When the Japanese first occupied Manila, they hoped to convince the Filipinos that they were their liberators. So they didn't imprison the missionaries for any length of time. They picked us up, kept us about ten days in Santo Tomas, then released us, under house arrest.

The night before our release, word came around "Tomorrow morning at 9:00 all missionaries line up in front of the Administration building." Many of us were housed there. Paul remembers looking up all his friends and acquaintances to say goodbye because he had no idea what would happen to us the next day. Were we all going to be taken out and shot, or what? Next morning we lined up in front of the building. Then we waited and waited and waited. Finally, about noon or thereafter they gave us instructions. "All missionaries are free to go home to your Mission compounds and continue your mission work, but don't have any contact with the Filipinos." "How do they think we can work without contact with the Filipinos?" Paul mused, "Do they think we are like nuns in a convent, praying for everybody, but not having any contact with anybody." We chuckled over that, paid attention to the first admonition, and ignored the second. We had plenty of contact with Filipinos.

Our quasi freedom under house arrest was just propaganda. We were confined to the house, except when one or another of us wore an arm band to go out to a store. But we were not able to carry on our work. Beyond the propaganda incentive for our release, it may be that the Religious Section of the Japanese army was sincere in wanting to treat the missionaries well. They were in the Japanese army, but as representatives of the Christian Church in Japan. Some of our later experiences supported that conclusion.

CHAPTER TWO

LOVE IN THE CRUCIBLE

The Japanese told us "Your friends will take care of you." That turned out to be true, but it was not that simple. There were 70 people in our compound during the house arrest period. The banks were closed. No communication with the source of our financial support in America, and I had to get food for all 70. We realized that we were on our own. The Japanese provided no rations, except some matches, a little salt, sugar, seasonings and that kind of thing. No basics. No rice. I had to scrounge for that. We began to figure. How were we going to get money?

Fortunately our Mission Board had a system of payment that none of the other missions had. We knew how much our appropriations were for the year, and the Board provided us with a book of drafts. Instead of waiting for a draft to come in the mail, as all the other missions did, we could write drafts at our own initiative, within the amount of our appropriations. So I had this book of drafts when the war broke. That gave us a splendid advantage. We could sell drafts to merchants who had been accumulating money.

Just before the war, when the likelihood of war was in the offing, the Chinese merchants in Manila had stocked up very heavily. They imported a lot of stuff. Flour was abundant when the war broke. I remember the amount of bread that was on the market for weeks after the war started. Vendors went around the streets, selling their wares. I remember one of them shouting, "White bread, brown bread, damn that Japanese red." That was the kind of thing that we heard in the streets. And the grocery stores were well stocked.

The merchants were selling their merchandise for Japanese occupation money. They were making money which they wanted to put it into safekeeping. So they sold it to us at quite a discount for drafts that they counted on being valid after the war. And we did not disappoint them. They hid the drafts under the floor or wherever they could and waited till the war was over. I kept a record of each transaction in a code book without any names, but with a code for each business man that brought money. That code book later figured in some risk to my life. After the war we redeemed the drafts, and put them through the bank.

Because the other missionaries had to wait for their payments to come by mail, they were cut off. The 70 people on our compound were not all Presbyterians. There were several other missions that had no way to get money. They were helpless. I had to get money for them.

My responsibility was to sell these drafts, dated before Pearl Harbor to protect our merchant friends as much as possible. For each transaction we would agree upon an exchange rate, and they would give me Japanese war money. Our rate of exchange would take into account the galloping inflation. We were under house arrest for two-and-a-half years, from mid January of 1942 to July of 1944. With inflation going up, it really was hard to get enough money to buy the food we needed. Just before the Americans got back, a pound of pork cost 400 pesos, or $200 in the prewar rate of exchange. Naturally we were not buying pork. An egg went for $35. We were not buying eggs. Toward the end, even a coconut cost as much as five dollars.

In order to get money, somehow I had to make contact with people who could provide it. So Alexander Christie and I ventured out for the first time. He had been appointed to replace me as Treasurer, but he had arrived in Manila only a week before Pearl Harbor. Nobody knew him. He had established his credentials with the bank and his signature was valid there, but the bank wasn't operating. He was so new that, in the emergency of war, people with whom I had dealt as treasurer required my joint signature with his, whenever we sold a draft. They didn't know him at all. It was his signature that validated the checks. Mine was the reassuring signature.

Wearing our arm bands, Alex and I went down town to a Chinese drug store, owned by a very fine Christian. We hoped he could let us have some money on a draft. Before I could tell him why we were there, he said, "You go into that back room here." We waited and waited ten minutes or 15 minutes, I guess. It felt like half an hour. He wanted to make certain no one had seen us. When he found that everything was secure he came in and handed us a bunch of bills. We started to count them. He said, "Don't count! Don't count! Take it and get out! We can take care of it later." He didn't want to get caught harboring Americans. We got the money, went home, counted it and saw that he got the draft for it. That was the start.

From then on, merchants would come to us with Japanese occupation currency. We bought food in the market and, as was common in Manila, from vendors who brought food to the door. Often, when our Chinese friends brought the money, they would come to our back door with a basket of vegetables. In that basket there would be a butter carton stuffed with bills, so they wouldn't be caught bringing money to us. We had butter cartons, about four inches square, just enough that they could stack the bills in them.

The Japanese had taken over our high school, across the street, for a hospital. Our house was easily visible, if they wanted to see what was happening. Fortunately, a huge acacia tree at our back door, more or less hid our visitors. In my apartment today I still have a very interesting table made from a section of tree trunk. It was from that tree that stood by our back door. That table is very meaningful to me, because the tree protected our transactions.

The merchants would come in our back door and into our bedroom. With the windows closed and the curtains all drawn, we would count the money and figure out a rate of exchange. Then we would give them a draft, dating it before the war, to protect them. Then they would sneak out.

I hid the money behind our sliding windows. The shell panes in those windows let light through but you couldn't see through them. There was a certain amount of space between those windows. I tied the money in bundles, with a nail stuck into the cross hatch on the outside of one window. I then pulled the other window over it so no one could see the money either from inside or out. For nearly two years, during this period of house arrest, we financed the living of those 70 people that way. One day as Viola and I sat in the living room, a Japanese soldier came to the door. We let him in. He said, "My commanding officer has ordered me to find out where you are getting your money." What could I say to him? I didn't want to betray the people who were bringing us money. I didn't know what to do. While I was trying to think what to say, he got up, went over to the piano and began to play hymns.

We visited a little. He never asked that question again, and left after a while. He sympathized with us, but was doing his duty to ask. What report he gave them, I didn't know. He probably fabricated something. In any case, he just took over the responsibility and used his imagination. That was it.

We had other contacts with our questioner. Johnny Fujita was a YMCA secretary in Japan who had been assigned to the Religious Section of the army. One Sunday in Ellinwood Church Fujita preached on love. He must have looked very carefully over the congregation to make certain that no officer was listening to him. Then he said, "I love you." Love in the crucible of war had found a way to bridge the boundaries of race and nation, and the enmity of war.

In New York, right after the war, I was attending a conference in the Riverside Church. I looked across the assembly room and saw Johnny Fujita. As soon as there was a break in the meeting we rushed together and embraced each other. He really was a very fine Christian and a good friend.

When we had our contacts with Johnny Fujita in Manila we knew little about his background. Nor did we know the other risks he felt called upon to take as a representative of the Imperial Japanese Army.

⋆⋅⧉⋅ ⧉⋅⋆

The following indented information, was secured after the death of Stephen L. Smith from Johnny Fujita, who was then serving as pastor of a Methodist congregation in southern California. Some details were also secured from Richard Terrill Baker, <u>Darkness of the Sun</u>, The Story of Christianity in the Japanese Empire, Abingdon Cokesbury Press, New York, Nashville 1947.

It now is known that the Rev. Mr. Fujita graduated from a theological seminary in Japan and received his Master of Theology degree from Drew Theological Seminary in Madison, New Jersey. While in the U.S. he married a Nisei (an American born Japanese) from Washington State. Not long before the war, he and his bride had arrived in Japan, where he became the Y.M.C.A. secretary in Tokyo. Mrs. Fujita had a difficult time in Japan, since she did not speak Japanese fluently, and was an American citizen. All during the war she was treated as an enemy alien, and was followed continuously by secret service agents.

Twenty days before Pearl Harbor the Rev. Jonathan Fujita was drafted into the Religious Section of the Propaganda Corps. That Corps consisted of as many as four or five hundred priests, ministers, announcers, musicians, journalists, photographers, artists and other communicators. It was a civilian unit attached to the Japanese Army that was to invade the Philippines. Although Fujita and the 25 other Protestant and Catholic clergy were technically civilians, they were given uniforms, guns and helmets and received brief basic training in military discipline.

The day before Christmas 1941, shortly after the beachhead had been secured, they landed in Lingayen on the island of Luzon. The Religious Section was instructed to protect the property and further the worship of the Philippine churches. They were the principal point of contact between the Japanese military and the churches. They were to discredit the missionaries and to make clear that Japan was not fighting the Philippines, but America. All the Protestant churches were to be united into one church. Through the pulpit and all their contacts they were to make clear that Japan was liberating the Philippines and ushering in a new era of the co-prosperity sphere.

Some say, it was the Religious Section that was responsible for convincing the military to release the missionaries from Santo Tomas. Many of Fujita's colleagues in the religious section carried out their instructions faithfully. Their leaders were not popular among their Filipino colleagues because of their anti-American propaganda. But Johnny, and at least one other, found themselves repeatedly in situations where they were able to ease the blow of the occupation on the missionaries and other religious workers for whom they had responsibility.

For example, when it came to the issue of money, Fujita said nothing about where the missionaries were getting money. Instead he told his superiors that the missionaries needed money. In the early days of the occupation the Propaganda Corps was given a good deal of priority by the high command, so he was given some money with which he was able to help some of the missionaries who were in particularly difficult circumstances.

Johnny Fujita was a good friend of Domingo Bascara, the Filipino Y.M.C.A. secretary. Bascara had been taken prisoner and was in Fort Santiago, where many of the enemies were tortured and executed. One night Fujita happened to be on duty at Fort Santiago. The other officers and soldiers there were either drunk or asleep when a messenger arrived with orders for Domingo Bascara and an American colleague to be executed. Fujita "lost" the order, and was subsequently jailed for eight days, for his carelessness. But the two prisoners lived to survive the war.

When it became clear that the Religious Section had largely failed in its mission, most of its members were sent back to Japan. Johnny Fujita was assigned to translate American broadcasts for the Imperial Japanese Navy. At the time people were being told that Japan was winning the war. So, when Fujita told clergy colleagues that Japan was losing the war, he was imprisoned for the duration of the conflict, and suffered some of the same privations enemy prisoners suffered.

--⊨⊙ ⊙⊫--

I had encounters with other members of the Religious Section. One day an officer came, and said, "We know that you are grateful for what we are doing for you. We'd like to have you write a letter of appreciation." There again I was stumped. What could I do? We were glad that they let us live at home. But, they wanted to publish the letter. And so, as I waited for his return, I had my little bag packed, ready to go to Bilibid, the concentration place. When he came back to get my letter, I said, "I'm afraid I can't give you a letter like that."

As we negotiated a little, he recalled that I had written a letter thanking them for releasing our Doctor McAnlis who had been in prison. It was a very simple expression of appreciation for that. He said, "I'll tell you what. How about that letter? Could we use that?" I replied, "Well it's your property. I'm not writing anything particularly now. You have it." But they never did use it. I don't know exactly how he got out of it. I'm sure he had a little squirming to do. He also, was a friend.

Prices kept going up. We couldn't eat very well. But one thing was always available: Fleischmann's Yeast. That was one commodity that did not advance in price. San Miguel Brewery was overproducing Fleischmann's yeast, and there wasn't much sale for it. While the price of beer and everything else went up, Fleischmann's yeast stayed at 25 centavos a pound. That would be twelve and a half cents in prewar money. It didn't change even with inflation, all that time we were in Manila. So we were able to get 50 pounds of yeast every Monday and divide it.

I happened to get a bicycle. A donor had shipped it to Manila for some Filipino evangelist down in the south. Of course when the war came we couldn't get it to him. I set it up and used it all during that period.

Every Monday morning I would ride my bicycle down to the San Miguel Brewery and place an order for the yeast and pay for it. Then I would go back in the afternoon to pick it up. On the way home, I left some of the yeast with the Methodists in their compound. One pound I took to a Jewish Cantor, who lived about two blocks from us. The rest of it I shared with the seventy people in our compound. We just ate the yeast like you would eat cheese. It had kind of a chalky taste, and wasn't too bad. We considered we were getting some protein we couldn't get any other way. It probably had some vitamins, too. We couldn't get much meat.

One day I was going back to pick up the yeast that I had paid for that morning. Near the brewery, some men were digging an air raid shelter for the military. A Japanese soldier was supervising them. The Filipino guard at the gate looked over and made certain that the Japanese soldier didn't see me. This Filipino drew to attention and saluted me, saying, "When are they coming?"

As the war progressed everybody "knew" a lot more than they really knew. One day, after the war, Paul came up with an interesting explanation for the way in which rumors would get started, while we were in captivity. He said,

> People generate rumors as a way to keep their spirits up and to have hope. You have to have hope or you get discouraged and give up. A lot of people that died more easily than others in the concentration camp were those that were not able to maintain their hope. You would hope and hope, and wait and wait, but nothing happened. People got discouraged. "Our country doesn't care about us," they would say. "Surely they would have come in the first few days." Later, as the weeks stretched out, we thought "Well a few more weeks. They've got to regroup. After all they had a bad loss at Pearl Harbor." So you rationalize and put it together with any scrap of information and any rumors that come around, and build hope on it. Then you try to be as objective as possible, looking at various sets of rumors, and deciding which are outrageously unreal and which might just possibly be true.

Aside from going for that yeast and shopping for the group, I had a lot of time on my hands. One thing I did do during the period of house arrest, I read the Tagalog New Testament through about 12 times. I got a quite good smattering of Tagalog that way. I could have learned to preach in it fairly soon, because I had a fair foundation then. But, I never did use it much, because English was so widely spoken and my work was more administrative than promotional. Interestingly enough, what I learned has stayed with me over the years. Even now, I can almost think in Tagalog. From high school days, language has always intrigued me.

Under house arrest, one has much time to think. In the crucible of war, one's whole life sometimes flashes before one's eye. I knew then, what I have come to treasure dearly. God's hand had been with us through years of preparation and throughout Viola's and my earliest ministry in the Philippines. But that is another story.

CHAPTER THREE

LIFE IN THE CRUCIBLE

American soldiers, as prisoners of war, were pressed into service by the Japanese. One group was loading grain onto a truck and riding with it under armed guard to unload it at their destination. As they were going down Dewey Boulevard, along the waterfront, they saw some pretty girls. One of the men grabbed the gun from the guard and waved it so the girls could see it, then handed it back to him. What could the guard do? He never should have let him get that gun at all. He was thinking of himself so he didn't do a thing. I suppose he may have been one of their raw recruits. By that time they had their best troops elsewhere where the fighting was going on. And some of the soldiers who were occupying the city were not very well trained.

As we found ourselves restricted under house arrest, our community found many different ways to go on living as creatively as possible, under the circumstances.

The people in our compound ate in several different dinning areas. At our house we had the Smith's and the MacDonalds and the Hayeses eating together. The Hayeses and the MacDonalds lived over in the Ellinwood Girls' School, on Tennessee Street, the other side of the Buchers. It was being used as a dormitory. There was a man's mess down in the lobby at Ellinwood. That included several doctors from China, and other men whose families were not with them. Alex Christie was in that mess. There was a mess at the Buchers, and one over at the Bousman's, who lived in the manse behind Ellinwood Church, next door to the high school.

Every Friday night we would close one of the messes and spread those people around to the other messes. Friday was party night. We would play games and have fun together. One of the doctors from China introduced us to a new game. We had a whole bunch of wooden mice carved out. Each person had a string attached to a mouse out in the middle of the table. The mice were all bunched together. The person who was "It" would try to capture as many of the mice as possible by putting a pan down onto the table. As soon as you saw that coming you would give your string a little jerk and pull your mouse away. If you were captured three times, you would be "It." We played all sorts of other games that people would remember or think up. This would not just be the young people, but everybody that would play together. That was our social life. On one of those social occasions, if Paul wanted to get a corsage for one of the girls, he would walk over to a nursery a few blocks away, wearing his arm band of course. They had big butterfly orchids for ten centavos, or you could get the small orchids for three centavos. So three of those plus a centavo for some lacy ferns, and they would put together a quite nice corsage for 10 centavos. What a contrast to the cost of food!

On Sunday we would go to church across the street in the Ellinwood Church. Viola was directing the choir there, part of the time at least, and giving organ lessons.

As one might expect, there were shortages of many things. For example, it was very difficult to get light bulbs. So Paul learned how to repair old ones. It was not easy and he sometimes failed, but many times he did succeed. To do so he had to see the broken filament. The frosted bulbs were more difficult, because he had to have enough clear glass to see the filament. But he found that between the frosty part and the metal there usually was a little bit of clear glass through which he could see the filament. He would screw the bulb into an extension cord, ready to apply current to it. He put a bright light behind it, and looked in to see the filament. Then, by tipping the bulb around and tapping it, he would get the broken ends together. If he succeeded in that he would turn on the power. They would arc and weld themselves together. After careful cooling they could be used. Amazingly, they lasted pretty well sometimes. Some would last for a day or two and sometimes they would go for weeks before they would burn out again.

Paul was rather ingenious about many things. One night we all slept through a robbery. As with almost all windows in Manila, our windows were covered with bars. But our screen porch was vulnerable. I had put a switch on the front door so it would ring an alarm bell if anyone opened it after the switch had been thrown. But the robbers simply slitted the screen, came through the hole and stole my portable typewriter, several light bulbs and some other things.

We knew that if they robbed a place once, they would usually come back, to see what else they could get. We sewed up the slit in the screen and Paul electrified it. If anyone tried to cut the screen again, they would get a jolt, or if they knew enough electricity to ground the screen, then a bright light would go on and the bell would ring. We had no further burglaries.

The young people on our compound found many different ways to occupy themselves. The red arm bands we were required to wear had a Japanese character for "Rice Man." That is what they called Caucasians, because we were like the color of rice. Our young people discovered that if you put the arm band upside down, it looked a little like an American eagle flying. So, with considerable glee they would wear them upside down. They figured that the Japanese would simply conclude that "These crazy Americans wouldn't know how to read or write anyway."

Young people don't hesitate to take risks when an opportunity for fun comes along. And parents often find out about their pranks long after they have taken place. Paul was no exception. As the Fourth of July was approaching, Paul decided he would have a special celebration. He had several packages of Chinese firecrackers. Before the war he had devised a way to make a little noisy bomb. This he did again. He selected one firecracker that had a particularly heavy fuse and peeled off all the outer layers of paper. He wanted to get as close as possible to only one layer of light brown paper, covering the inner part of the firecracker. Then he surrounded that firecracker with several layers of other firecrackers that he had peeled down in the same manner. Finally he wrapped all of them with heavy string until it was a really good little ball.

He made time fuses by soaking cotton string in a saturated solution of potassium nitrate and drying it carefully, so as to insure an even burn.

With a stop watch, he tested the fuse, to calculate how long a fuse he would need for whatever time he wanted.

Long before the Fourth, Paul made two of these noisy bombs with fuses long enough to burn for the length of time it took Paul to walk, without hurrying, the one block from our house up to the corner of Taft Avenue, a very busy thoroughfare. He added an extra few seconds on them in case of miscalculation.

The Fourth finally came. Paul took the two bombs with their time fuses and went up to Taft Avenue, about a block from our house. He saw that there were no soldiers around or anybody watching too closely. So he lifted up the grate on the storm drain, let down one of the bombs, and brought the fuse up through the grate, tying it so it wouldn't drop clear down out of his reach. He put the grate back down, walked across Tennessee to the other grate, and did the same. Then he sat down on the curb and watched the traffic.

Timing the traffic, Paul discovered that the length of time he had on his fuse, was almost the same as it took inbound traffic to reach this corner, from the circle he could see way out on Taft Avenue. Paul waited patiently. Finally, he saw three truck loads of soldiers coming down Taft Avenue. As they rounded the rotunda coming in his direction, he lit the first fuse, walked across the street, lit the second fuse, and sauntered on home. He got inside our fence, hid behind a bush and watched.

Just as the first truck appeared at the intersection his first bomb went off. Boom. It reverberated. There was a screeching of brakes and the tail end of the first truck was just barely visible down the sidewalk. The second and third trucks came into the intersection. All the soldiers came piling out of their trucks with guns at the ready. About that time the second bomb went off. Boom! The soldiers whirled about to find out who was attacking them. "It was only little old me," he liked to say in telling about it. The soldiers couldn't find anybody, so eventually they got back in their trucks and proceeded to wherever they were going.

"That was a real Fourth of July celebration!" Paul bragged. "I wonder what kind of thing was going through their heads. They probably made no connection with the Fourth of July. But I sure did." Then justifying himself, "Fun loving kids will always find ways to have fun. Oh yes, it was a little dangerous to pull that stunt, but life isn't any fun if you don't engage in a little bit of danger."

Well there was danger enough and to spare.

As I said, we had decided earlier that we wouldn't try to go out into the country side to run away. We would wait and see what came. We figured that the commanding officers in Manila would be more responsible people than some of the subordinates that we might encounter outside. Some of the people who ran away to the mountains were killed. We stayed in Manila, but we did have a few contacts with the guerrillas.

Norman Reyes, one of Paul's buddies at the radio station, went with the army when they evacuated Manila. He and Leone Ma Guerrero, who was known on the air as Ignacio Javier, were the Voice of Freedom out on Bataan. After Bataan fell, they went to Corregidor and were the Voice of Freedom there, until the Japanese took Corregidor. One day, before Bataan fell, Norman Reyes suddenly appeared at our house. Paul surely had not expected to see him. But there he was. He had come cross country from Bataan avoiding the roads, and crossing the fields. He told us that on the way he had to kill a Japanese soldier. He had come, he said, to ask Paul for some headphones. They were in short supply and the army needed some. Paul had two or three pairs in his room so he gave him a couple of sets. Norman took them and returned to Bataan. That was Paul's little contribution to the Voice of Freedom.

During the house arrest period, Mary Boyd Stagg, pastor of the Cosmopolitan Church and others in the congregation, were helping the Filipino guerrillas. Somebody infiltrated their number and the Japanese came suddenly to pick her up. It happened that young Sam Boyd Stagg, Mary's son, was out with his bicycle at the time the Japanese came to pick up his family. He was visiting Paul, who was a good friend. Sam was at our house several blocks from the Church when he heard the news of it. We advised him to go back and be with his family. We felt that if they caught him later and knew who he was, it would be harder on him. He went home, and was picked up with his family. Sometime later the soldiers tortured and beheaded his mother along with several others. But he survived.

We had a couple of other contacts with the guerrillas. Only once during the entire course of the war were we able to get some word to our sons in California via the Red Cross. But we did have another offer to communicate with them which we turned down. We decided against it because we might get caught. Whether that was a bona fide offer, I don't know.

A Colonel in the guerrillas, whom we knew, came asking for an American flag. She wanted it to display on a hill slope as a signal to guide our submarines. They would indicate by standing in one corner or another whether it was safe for the sub to come in. We had a flag in our chest, and debated quite a bit before deciding to give it to her. It had my name on it. So with some indelible ink I completely obliterated the name and gave it to her.

We wrapped the flag in some yellow cloth and made a very neat long package which she fastened on the inside of her thigh. She got through with it and she brought the flag back after the war. I wish I had saved it.

The Japanese military made periodic unannounced inspections. It didn't seem like it was very often. It may have been once a quarter but it didn't seem very regular either. It was kind of a spot check.

During these visits, we were concerned about Paul. Because he had been a radio announcer, and had taken great delight in jamming their radio station, he was a marked man. Throughout our period of house arrest, one of our fears was that they might recognize him.

Paul was 18 years old. Like many young people his age, he was very interested in communication equipment. His room was filled with all kinds of radios, sets he was rebuilding, and things like that. He had an old radio which had both short wave and standard broadcast bands. The Japanese did not want anyone listening to short wave radio. So at first, in order to be able to do that, Paul rigged it so he could turn the volume way up and listen to the broadcast band, then turn it way down and listen to short wave on headphones.

But then the authorities started going around with a truck with a directional antenna on top of it, listening for short wave oscillator frequencies. When they would pick up one of these frequencies they would zero in on it and confiscate the radio.

Finally the authorities called all radios in, and removed the short wave parts from all of them so you couldn't tune in short wave any more. In the Philippines, before the war, all radios had been registered. The Japanese had those lists, so there was no escape. We had to bring them in.

But Paul had some old radio parts that once had been a working radio. So he tried to build a short wave radio set in a cigar box. Outside the box was a power supply which he took from a regular radio. He never did get that radio to work. But there it was sitting on the shelf between a couple of other cigar boxes and odds and ends of nuts and bolts, and whatever. Paul had all kinds of junk in that room. He had a turn table and a simulated radio studio to practice on.

We trembled every time an inspection came. We were afraid they might go into his room and find all that equipment, and he would be in deep trouble. If they had found that turn table they might have thought Paul was broadcasting. There is no telling what they might have done with him.

But providentially, they never once went into that room. His room was really an open screened porch. It had no windows, just curtains. I guess that's what threw them off. They would go to our medicine chest and examine everything, and open drawers and look everywhere. But never once did they go into that room. It was amazing!

And they didn't know where we hid our money either. In all their searching, they never once discovered that.

Before long, we realized that we needed to set up a school for the children of our community. At first we had 11 children in school. Six more arrived when the missionaries were brought in from the mountains, in southern Luzon, where they had been hiding. Two or three others came from off the compound. They all went to school for a normal school day.

In the high school group we must have had more than a half dozen young people. They profited from a considerable number of very good teachers, many of whom had been displaced from China. Barbara Hayes was excellent for English literature. An Episcopal missionary taught them civics. And a Phi Beta Kappa from China was their history teacher. He was a prolific reader, among other things. First aid was taught by Dr. McAnlis. Alex Christie taught Bible.

One of the young people in our school was Reuben Shay, a German Jewish friend of Paul's. He wanted to spend time with our young people on the compound but didn't want to get us in trouble. So he went to the Japanese authorities and said, "Although my father was German and my mother was French, I am planning to become an American after the war, and I wish to associate with my American friends from school. If you wish to put me in prison that would be acceptable, but I would like to associate with a group on the Mission Compound near my house." The authorities respected his forthrightness. So they gave him a special paper in both Japanese and English that permitted him to spend time with us. He carried that, and came to school every day.

Reuben wanted to set up an underground Scout troop. Paul, as the oldest in our group, helped him organize it. Reuben served as scout master, and the two of them each headed a patrol. The scouts needed uniforms and badges. None were available for sale. So, each scout had to get his mother to make them or he had to make his own. Paul embroidered his own first class badge with meticulous attention to detail.

Their scout troop met in one of the rooms at the Ellinwood Girls School where they had their regular school classes. One day, as they were meeting, all decked out in their uniforms with their merit badge sashes on, someone came rushing in and cried, "The Japanese are on their way to inspect the building." There wasn't any place to go to get out of the way fast enough, and they couldn't get to wherever their quarters were, to get out of their uniforms. So they all piled into the closet where they kept their troop things and their U.S. flag.

They grabbed up all their things and packed themselves in there like sardines, locked the door and kept perfectly quiet. They could hear the soldiers going around looking at this and that. Pointing to their door, the soldiers asked, "How about this?" "Oh that's just an old closet," someone replied, "Nobody seems to know where the key is for that." But of course, at that point, the key was on the inside of the door to lock it. In reality anyone could use an ordinary skeleton key to open it. But fortunately they didn't push too hard to look in there. They asked two or three times, then gave up and went on. There were many pounding hearts in that closet. It could have been very bad for them if they had been found in those uniforms. The inspection may have lasted no more than ten or fifteen minutes. But it was pretty crowded and pretty hot. Eventually somebody came back and said, "They're gone." So a bunch of frightened scouts came out and finished their meeting.

Working on various merit badges led to a good deal of creative activity.

As part of their cooking merit badge the scouts had to be able to use a kitchen as well as to cook out doors. The ovens were not working because we couldn't keep a pilot light going. The gas we were getting during the war was made from charcoal and was very dirty. We could clean the top burners fairly easily, but it became impossible to keep the ovens going. People next doors had an electrolux gas refrigerator. I think Paul had to clean it once a month for a while. Eventually they gave up on it. And we gave up using the oven in our house.

To replace our oven, Paul made one with an old electric burner, the kids had found in a field. He put it in a five-gallon kerosene can and spread clay-like mud around the can. As their cooking project the boys baked a cake in that oven. We didn't have any wheat flower. A cake made with rice flour alone would fall apart. So they mixed rice flour with cassava flour and experimented until they found the right proportion. When they got the right combination it would hang together rather well and had a fairly good texture. Chicken eggs were very expensive and hard to come by. Duck eggs were fairly plentiful and relatively cheap. So they used duck eggs. They would take the whites from two duck eggs for the frosting, cooking them with sugar in the top of a double boiler. They would use the yolks plus another duck egg as part of the cake mix. It worked well.

For their Physical Development badge, the group made a volleyball court, and each of them took turns officiating. There were tennis courts near the church and they played quite a bit of tennis. For their rope climbing, they hung a rope from a big tree between the manse and the church. That was right next to our high school, which the Japanese were using as an auxiliary hospital. The lesser wounded, or those who were sick, with something like malaria, were cared for there.

When our boys were not climbing the rope, they loved watching the Japanese wrestling matches, which took place inside a circle. If any part of a wrestler other than his feet or hands touched the ground, he was out. Or if any part of his body, including his feet, touched outside the circle, he lost.

Paul was especially fascinated with a small fellow, who always seemed to win. He was very strong and could take some of the heavy ones, grab their fandoshe, lift them up in the air, walk over to the edge, and set them down outside the circle. It was very seldom that anybody could throw him. If he could get to them, he would keep winning. He would then take his place back in line of those waiting for another turn in the circle.

One time Paul was doing rope climbing, hand over hand up to the limb of the tree and then coming back down. Across the fence, an old Japanese soldier was watching him. When Paul came down, the soldier got his attention and said, "You come!" Paul went over to see what he wanted. The old man asked, "How old you?" Paul replied, "I'm 18." Paul had a full black beard. "Hard to believe," said the soldier, "Me think you older." "No," Paul insisted, "I'm 18." "Me think you are 21." Paul said, "No, I'm 18." The old man asked, "How old you think I?" Well, Paul didn't know what might offend the old fellow, guessing too low or too high, so he never did guess.

The old man was shaved bald and was kind of a tubby old fellow. He grew serious and began to talk in earnest. "You know, me very old soldier. Fight in many war. Fight in Manchuria. Fight in Korea. Fight in China. Now fight in Philippines."

About that time they heard the big guns. Bataan had already fallen and they were shooting at each other across the straits between Corregidor and Bataan. The aged warrior paused a moment to listen. Then he went on. "You know, in Bataan many soldier die. Many Filipino soldier die. Many American soldier die. Many Japanese soldier die. I sorry!"

Here was a crusty old veteran. You would think he would be about as calloused as you could get. He had been trained in Bushido and had been doing all this fighting, wars, after war, after war. You would think he would be about as hard-bitten as they come. Yet he deeply cared about human life, whether it was his or someone else's. Here was a real human being, touched with sorrow for all that killing.

When Paul got back to the States, people couldn't understand why he didn't hate the Japanese, after all he had been through. Then Paul would tell them that story. Closing with tears in his eyes and maybe a little break in his voice, he would say, "You cannot condemn a whole group of people for what some of that group do. It's just not fair. It's not reasonable. It just doesn't hold. People are people. Every person is an individual, and needs to be treated as such."

CHAPTER FOUR

THE CRUCIBLE HEATS UP

In July 1944 things were reaching a critical point. We had been under house arrest for about two-and-a-half years. Change was in the air. Somehow we realized, nothing could go on as it was. We were not really aware of it at the time, but the U.S. forces were at the height of their hedgehopping. Nearly eight months later we would be rescued rather dramatically. But that is getting ahead of our story. One thing we had discovered, the Japanese usually made their moves on the eighth of the month, because that was the date of the Emperor's birthday. So, whenever change seemed to be immanent, we would expect it on the eighth. Consequently, we were always prepared.

On July 8, 1944, we were waiting for something. And it happened! That day soldiers came in the evening and told us, "We'll come for you tomorrow and take you to a place of safety. You get ready. You may take two suitcases, and we will come and get you in the morning."

All night we prepared. We had stored food in our house. In our bedroom we had a couple of big bins four or five feet square full of rice. We were able to get a lot of rice early in the occupation. We mixed it with lime to keep the weevils out. When we were ready to eat it, we'd take some of that rice, wash the lime out of it, and cook it. Also, we had some other food hanging from the ceiling. We couldn't take it with us, so we let our servants help themselves to it during the night.

We spent the whole night getting our suitcases ready. We didn't sleep at all. We had our stuff all packed and waiting when the time came. I had a duffel bag and a suitcase. Among other things, I had a couple of pairs of shoes in that duffel bag. While we were waiting for the soldiers to come, somebody stole the duffel bag. So during the whole time in the concentration camp at Los Baños, I wore some wooden shoes. They were too short for me so I developed a spur on the heel and had to have surgery on it after the war.

By the way, ever since my high school class in etymology, the origin of words has always fascinated me. Wooden shoes, like they have in Holland, are called "sabot." When a sabot, or wooden shoe, was thrown into the enemy's machinery to destroy it, that was called "sabotage." And that's the origin of our word sabotage.

This time, when the soldiers arrived, they had an interpreter with them. He was probably a Korean or Taiwanese. He spoke very good English, having gone to school in the States, and was reasonably friendly. All missionaries were to be picked up this time. None were to be left behind. They took us directly to Santo Tomas, a Roman Catholic University, that was being used as a concentration camp. We were not allowed to mingle with others there. Our captors had set up tents in the front lawn between the gate and the buildings. They put some of us in those tents overnight. Others, they took to the gymnasium. We spent the whole day and part of the night there on the gymnasium floor.

Then around three in the morning they took all of us to the railroad station, and put us on board a train, in regular third class coaches. They took us to the Los Baños station and up to the internment camp, before it was light. They didn't want the Filipinos to know about our movements.

The camp had been in use for some time. Everything was ready. It was located on the grounds of an agricultural school that had also been used as a military installation. There were some dormitories and some barracks there. We found out later that there were 2,146 of us living in about 26 different barracks.

We were housed in a long barracks with wood framing and "sawali" walls, made of woven bamboo. A peaked nipa thatch roof ran the length of the building. Usually two people were housed in an eight by 10-foot cubicle. Each barracks had 48 cubicles, 24 on each side of a 4-foot wide hall, which ran the length of the building. Across the middle of the building was another hall about 6 feet wide. So the two hallways divided the barracks into four quadrants with 12 cubicles in each quadrant.

Each cubicle was provided with two single-width metal folding cots with flat springs and mattress pads about two-and-a-half inches thick. If you put the head of the beds at the outer wall of the cubicle, you would have approximately three feet between the end of the beds and the hallway wall. There were about two-and-a-half feet between the beds. The cubicles were partitioned with sawali walls, like the exterior walls of the barracks. There was an open door to the hallway covered with a curtain.

If you wanted a shelf you had to build it yourself, provided you could find the materials. People modified their cubicles to suit their styles of living. As time went on, quite a few people created a doorway in their side wall, so they could go right out of the building, without going through the halls.

At the end of each building there was an entrance. But the way we walked through the compound was through the middle of the barracks. A passage way connected the middle of each pair of dormitories. That connection passed through the middle of a shed, which contained our toilet and bath facilities, such as they were. On one end of the shed, to the right of the passage way as we went to the next barracks, were the men's showers and latrines. At the other end, to the left was the women's room. Going through the middle of that shed, it was hard to remember which way to turn. One day when Viola was bathing, a man came in. She jumped behind a screen before he saw her.

Viola had the unpleasant job of cleaning up the six hole women's latrine. About every ten minutes the whole thing would flush into a septic tank down an incline trough under the holes. Sometimes the accumulation of feces and toilet paper would dam up the flow, so it was kind of a mess. There was a time when we didn't have sufficient water. And of course the flushing of the latrines wasn't too good then either

All of the arriving internees were housed in a section of the camp separated completely from the rest of the camp by a fence. Our captors didn't want us to take any news we may have gleaned on the outside to the internees who had been in the camp for some time, at least until a couple of weeks had passed.   Then, anything we might bring them would be old news.

For a few days, food was brought to us from the main kitchen in a cart. Two or three fellows would push the cart up to our gate. They had to go through a guard post there.   Our food servers would meet them at the gate. When Paul went to pick up the food for our barracks, he saw Bert Fonger in the group that was pushing the cart up to us. He had known Bert at Bordner school, so they started to greet each other.   The guard cut them off abruptly, "No, No, No! No talk!"

The next time Bert was bringing up the cart for another meal, he stood there looking up into the sky. He kept his hands on the cart handle, ignoring Paul completely. Paul watched him. When Bert was sure Paul was paying attention to him, he quickly looked down to his hand and back up again. Once again he ignored Paul, but Paul got the message. So Paul slipped his hand over Bert's hand. Bert then pulled his hand out carefully, and Paul got the note which was hidden there. That was how they communicated with each other during that period.

During the time our camp was separated from the others, Paul noticed a couple of kids sitting with their backs to the fence that separated us from the main camp. He recognized one of them and wanted to talk to him. So Paul went into the barracks and came out the back into some tall grass. The guard could not see our side of the fence at that point, without coming through the gate. But the young people on the other side of the fence could see the guard as he stood in front of his post. Paul crawled through the tall grass into a ditch and came up to the fence. He made himself known and they conversed for a while. Suddenly, one of them said, "The guard's coming to look!" So Paul backed down into the ditch, and lay there very quietly. The guard looked in Paul's direction. Seeing nothing, he went back to his post at the gate. Paul went back up to the fence and continued the conversation.

A few days after our arrival they set us up with our own kitchen, separate from the main part of the camp. I was in charge of one of the dormitories and of its food line. We got only two meals a day. The first meal was between eight and ten o'clock in the morning, and the second about five or six p.m. Two men from our barracks would bring our meal from the kitchen in big army aluminum kettles, full of watery rice or liquid stew. Sometimes there would be a few leaves of vegetables in the stew. And once a week, until the pigs were gone, we had one pig for 2,147 people, to give a little pork. So if someone got a shred of pork he was lucky. It was pretty thoroughly minced up in it.

After we joined the main part of the camp, our particular food line had up to 120 people: 96 persons from our barracks along with some ex-internee guards that lived in the back of the barracks where the camp held some of its entertainment. We developed the reputation for being the best food line in camp, partly because of the method we worked out for even distribution of left overs.

Every food line tried their best to divide the available food equally among all internees. In spite of that, it was a difficult task to come out even. So, in our food line, we gave each person a little less than enough to use it up. Then we would divide whatever was left over into half-servings of seconds which we would give to as many as six or eight people after the line had gone through.

We worked out a plan of rotation for the left overs in each of four food categories: rice, stew, greens and mush for breakfast. Whatever was left over in any particular food category would be served in half servings in rotation to everyone in the barracks. A chart was kept on the bulletin board indicating who had received left overs for each food category and who was next. So that, in one category of food, the list might be half way down the barracks, and in another category two-thirds down the barracks. Each type of food was distributed evenly over the long haul.

One time when serving the stew, instead of coming out with one or two half servings left over, Paul came out about a half serving short. Our family had a way of guarding against that eventuality. A different quadrant of our barracks started the line each day. Either Viola or I would pick up the three portions for our family so we could eat together. However, to guard against a glitch, we did not start to eat until the food had all been served. So that day when Paul did run short, we simply took the missing half-portion out of our family serving and made that up to the family that came out short.

One time, the Japanese allowed a case or two of corned beef in a Red Cross shipment to come through to the camp. It went into the stew which was like soup. There may have been an average of about one shred per person. A shred was perhaps a 16th of an inch in diameter and a quarter of an inch long. On this occasion one family of two got three shreds of corned beef and another family of three got two shreds. That day we came about as close to an altercation over our food service as any time that I can recall. Paul was the server in the middle of it. But he had done the best he could and just had to sit there and take the hostility.

When we first arrived, the newcomers in the fenced off section of the camp, were nuns, priests and missionaries who had been under house arrest. Laughingly, we became known as the Holy City. That was a derisive term, in a way. But our experience demonstrated that there was much more truth than poetry in it.

Ours was a widely varied collection of Catholics and Protestants with important differences. But we came to appreciate each other's viewpoints and to make friendships that lasted beyond the war.

There were significant contrasts between the experiences of our Christian community, as varied as it was, and the main part of the camp, which was just a cross section of everybody from priests to prostitutes. They had the problems that most societies have. They had disputes that had to be arbitrated in some way. They had to set up a court. They had to have a jail. Of course we had problems too, but there was a difference.

During the early part of our stay at Los Baños the Japanese allowed Filipinos to bring food to the gate once a week. An internee committee was allowed to buy that food and then to resell it to anyone that had the money to buy it. There were canteens in both sections of the camp. The canteen in the main part of the camp had to be under lock and key and was guarded at all times. In the Holy City one of the nuns and I ran the canteen. It was in an empty barracks. The tables were set up. The food was laid out on the tables. The people came and bought. Whatever wasn't sold the first day was just left there. The next day it was still there at canteen time to sell. It had not been locked up at all. Nobody thought of stealing it.

Our food lines in the Holy City also were different. Practically all of the Seventh Day Adventists would not eat pork, under any circumstances, even when they were starving. When there was pork, we operated two separate food lines at our kitchen, one with pork and one without pork. So the Seventh Day Adventists could go through and have their non-pork meal. Those that wanted non-pork food could have that, and those who wanted pork could have that. We made accommodations in an effort to be reasonable to everyone. Do you think they would do that in the main part of the camp? No way!

Later when the camp was united, and food was brought from the main kitchen, there was no way we could differentiate. Food came, and if it had pork in it, some of the Seventh Day Adventists decided just to take the meat out of it, and eat the broth with everything else. They would give their meat to those who were willing to eat it. But some of them would not touch anything in which pork had been cooked.

CHAPTER FIVE

OVERWHELMING PRESSURE INTENSIFIES

Life was not easy in the concentration camp. To supply the fires in our kitchen, we had to get our own wood from the surrounding forest. At first we used to rotate the responsibility for the wood chopping. But the wood from those trees was quite resilient and difficult to chop. Your axe had to be very sharp and you had to be very strong. The Jesuit priests proved to be best at handling that chore, and they volunteered to do the wood chopping. We turned it over to them. Then others would go out, barracks by barracks, and carry the wood to the kitchen.

When our separate kitchen was set up, Paul was assigned as breakfast cook. The stokers would go to the kitchen about 4:30 in the morning and start building the fires in the concrete fire boxes. Above them was a long continuous concrete block. Embedded in it was a series of oversized woks about a meter in diameter, each with a firebox under it.

Early in camp life our breakfast consisted of corn and rice mixed into a thin mush. To stir the food, the cooks had large 12 by 14 inch paddles with canoe length handles. While the cereal was cooking, they would stir constantly to keep it from sticking to the bottom of the wok and burning. It was rigorous physical work. Each cook was responsible for a couple of the woks next to each other. They would stir one. Then they would go over and stir the other. Then they would come back and stir the first one. Back and forth, over and over, they would go until both were almost cooked. They had some control over the flue so they could bank the fires when the cooking was complete.

One day Paul went out on a special detail to dig a new garbage pit. He was barefoot and wearing shorts, pretty much the same thing he had been wearing while cooking breakfast that morning. Then he stepped on something sharp. We never did figure out what caused the injury. He couldn't find anything. It may have been a big thorn. The doctors decided to give him a tetanus shot which nearly killed him. He was laid up in bed for several weeks.

When Paul began to get better, the doctors decided he should not go back to the strenuous work of stirring the breakfast woks. About that time the Holy City needed some electrical repair work. So Paul was assigned to be the Holy City camp electrician and was put in contact with the Japanese in charge of supplies. Poto-san was not very colorful or noteworthy, but not a bad guy, kind of a stodgy plodder. He might have done pretty well hauling a rickshaw. Namiki-san was much slighter of build, with big ears, and a wide smile. So everybody called him Mickey Mouse. Respectfully, Paul called him Namiki-san. He smiled if someone called him Mickey Mouse. He was just a jovial sort of character and very willing to help get whatever supplies that were needed.

One area in the kitchen needed more light. To make the corn and rice mush, the cooks needed corn that didn't have too many weevils in it. The ladies would sit at long tables under a dim light, going over the corn, trying to pick out the bugs and the weevils before the corn was mixed with the rice. With Namiki-san's help, Paul got wire and light bulbs and installed lights over the tables.

In spite of the good ladies work, our mush still had weevils in it. We would pick them out and lay them aside as we ate. But Paul got to thinking. "Shucks," he said one day, "The weevils are cooked and there is a tiny bit of protein there. Anyway, whenever I take a bite, there probably is a little worm hiding in there somewhere. I don't see it, so it never gets picked out. And I haven't had any problem with any of them. So the next one I see I'll go ahead and eat him." That is what Paul did, and it didn't taste any different. So he picked up the ones he had put aside that day, put them back in the mush, and stirred them in. He didn't bother picking any more out after that. Viola never was able to follow his example.

Paul went around and changed bulbs where they were burned out, and fixed wiring as necessary. He asked Namiki-san for more supplies whenever he needed them. When the soldiers went to Manila again for supplies of various sorts, they brought back bulbs and wire. Paul enjoyed being an electrician until the two sections of the camp were joined. Trained electricians from among the internees took over then.

Some time later, all that wire and Paul's tool box got him in trouble with the Japanese. They thought that Paul might have the short wave radio they were looking for, because there was a jewel light in his tool box. He was in danger of being "interrogated" when Paul Eldridge rescued him. Eldridge was the Seventh Day Adventist minister that used to do the morning devotional programs that first month of the war, so he knew Paul fairly well. Fortunately, he was in our barracks when they came for Paul. He spoke fluent Japanese, having been a missionary in Japan before he was assigned to the Philippines. So he was one of our major interpreters. He must have taken at least a half hour to talk the guards out of taking Paul for interrogation. He explained that Paul had been the electrician for that part of the camp. That was why he had those coils of wire in his room. That little jewel like thing was just one of the many things that he happened to have in his tool box from before the war and had no connection with anything. Eldridge finally convinced them and they left Paul alone.

The internal administration of the camp was in the hands of the Americans. The Japanese guarded the perimeter and controlled the amount of food we got. And of course, they were looking over our shoulders all the time and intervening when they felt it was necessary. Each barracks elected a monitor. All the monitors together formed a Central Committee which elected a chairman. The Central Committee made decisions for the whole camp and the chairman served as the principal liaison with the Japanese commandant.

Our democratic government operated under many unusual situations. Somewhere along the line, the Japanese decided that we were to make rope for the Japanese Navy, and told us so, through the Central Committee. The Central Committee told them, "We will let the people vote on that." Under the Geneva Convention, internees can undertake labor for pay if they wish to. But as we discussed it, we figured that this was something to help their armed services, and we did not want to do that.

43

The discussion went around all through the camp. Then each barracks voted. The vote in our barracks was 100% "No." The Central Committee got together and found that all the barracks had voted against the proposal. . I don't know if the vote in every barracks was unanimous, but at least the majority vote in each barracks was opposed. So the chairman went to the Japanese commandant and said, "No. They have voted that they will not do this. This would be working against our country. We will not do it." The word got back. O.K. No salt. So they cut off our supply of salt. I don't remember how long this lasted but it was long enough that we began to feel the effects of salt deprivation. We had begun to get used to the taste of the food without the salt. If you are hungry, you manage to eat the food without the salt. Eventually they gave in and let us have salt again, without our having to beg for it. They just decided that we meant business and we weren't going to do it, whatever threats they made.

The Central Committee assigned each internee to an appropriate task. There were wood choppers, stokers, cooks and food preparers, garbage details and all of the tasks that a small town might require. Paul was on the internee guard detail, scheduled most of the time from three to five in the morning. In between his cubicle and the one where we were located was the Secrest family. The mother with their youngest child was in the cubicle next to him. Across the aisle from them were the father and the older boy. The little child was still demanding a lot of baby type attention. The whole barracks was aware every morning when the little fellow would tune up and say, "Mommy, I want to wee wee." "Mommy, I want to wee wee." And it would get louder and louder until finally, mommy, who must have been a night person and not very fast at waking up in the morning, would finally give him some attention and help him go wee wee. Nobody wanted to complain about it. But in the repetition of this each morning, after Paul was just barely getting to sleep, eventually he lost all patience. Exasperated, he boomed out in his big bass voice, "Well, go ahead and wee! Your mommy can't do it for you!" This was greeted with tittering laughter throughout the whole barracks.

One morning, as our food rations were getting dangerously low, Paul was on the detail assigned to carry the breakfast mush from the kitchen to our barracks. He and the son of a Seventh Day Adventist doctor were carrying one of the big army aluminum kettles full of breakfast mush, each weighing about 25 pounds. It had been raining and the road was very slippery. Paul was the rear person on one of the pots. He had his left hand on the handle of the pot and his right hand on the shoulder of the person in front of him. They were slogging up through the mud which was about a foot deep. Some of the barracks had carts to carry their food and their carts would make deep ruts in the mud. Paul happened to step on the upper edge of one of those ruts and his foot slipped down into the rut. He lost his balance completely and the pot fell. The mush ran down Paul's arm, burned it, and went into the mud. But some of the mush stayed in the pot. Quickly they scooped up what they could without getting any dirt with it. One of the food detail who wasn't carrying anything at the time took over for Paul, and they went on ahead with the food that was remaining. It was measured and served out evenly in unusually small portions.

Someone else went back to the kitchen and got an empty pot and a shovel. So Paul and another fellow, who stayed behind, took the shovel and scooped up all the mush they could get that didn't include a lot of mud. This they dumped into the empty pot. The last shovel full was about half and half mud and mush so they didn't put it in the pot. Paul just carried that shovel separately. The other fellow carried the lightly loaded pot. They got up to the barracks and asked the doctors what to do with the mush that had dirt and gravel in it. The doctors said, "If anyone wants to eat the stuff, you guys picked up from the mud, they should boil it for half an hour. Then you can be sure its safe and you can eat it."

We found out how many people were interested in having the extra on those terms, and evenly divided the muddy mush as best we could. Paul brought us that last shovel full of mud and mush, and said, "Let's cook it and get some good out of it." We boiled it and tried to eat it. It had been cooked pretty thoroughly, so we didn't get any dysentery from it. Paul and I sat there picking out what pebbles we could, but we didn't get too far with it. It was very hard to be a chicken getting that gravel between our teeth. It wasn't very pleasant. Viola later told me that, as she sat there watching us, she felt more hatred than she had ever felt in her life.

We finally gave up on that gravely mixture, although we had swallowed a fair amount of it. We took the remains over to the next barracks where there was an Italian family that had some chickens they were raising. We gave it to the chickens. So it was not wasted.

In the midst of our hunger, all anyone could talk about was food. Women would sit around in the center of the barracks at night talking about recipes. Chocolate cake? How do you do this? How do you do that? The only light we had was in the sheltered part of the barracks where the lights were shaded. There were no lights in the cubicles themselves. So folks would sit around where the lights were and talk about food and recipes and so on.

As the food was getting shorter Albert Sanders, a seminary professor, taught a class in Logic on a collegiate level. Several young people joined the class. But they found that it really didn't matter what topic they were studying at the beginning of the class. By the end of the class they always ended by talking about food. It was inevitable. They tried to concentrate on the subject as long as they could, but finally the discussion came around to food.

One of the cooks was quite rotund and loved donuts. He would describe all kinds of ways to make donuts and what you could do with them. That kind of thing was going on all the time with different people in different situations.

Even when the food situation had became absolutely intolerable there were ways in which internees could get some extra food if they had the money to buy it from our captors. Some of the guards were selling rice for rings and other jewelry.

I had some U.S. currency that I took with me into camp and put it in a coffee can with a lid on it. I didn't realize there was a little crack around the lid. I hid the can in a hollow tree near our cubicle. Things were getting very tight along toward the end. There was a chance to buy some mongo beans, so that Viola could have some protein to add to the food we had and get a little better nourishment. I could get a little coffee can of lentils for $100 U.S. money.

I fished that can out of the hollow tree near our barracks. The termites had gotten into it and eaten up about half of it. When I saw it, I said, "Oh, I'm sick." For a moment, Viola was frightened because she thought I meant physically. Those bills were so destroyed that it looked as though about half of them were gone. Some of them were utterly no good. But I was able to piece together certain ones with the number showing and paste them on paper and if you had more then 50% you could get it replaced. Some of them were good and I got enough money to buy the lentils for us. I think it was for fifty dollars. The termites had eaten a fortune. And of course, if they had eaten more than half, it was theirs.

On Thanksgiving day we had one special meal with a little extra food. They killed two pigs for 2,147 people and the meat was minced up in the rice stew with some beans, I think. One of our missionaries got two little pieces of pork in his stew and one other didn't get any. Right there in the food line, a mature man broke down crying because he didn't get any meat. The strain was just overwhelming.

There was a lot of excitement on that Thanksgiving day as we were giving out the food. Roy Brown was quite nervous thinking about the special food. He came and shakily held his cup out. They put some in it, and he dropped it. It was a horrible thing to spill it. But the people in our food line all agreed that he could have another serving. That wouldn't have happened in any of the other barracks.

Lieutenant Konishi was supply officer, responsible for food supplies in our camp. He had been hated bitterly when he had similar responsibilities at Santo Tomas. His first act when arriving at Los Baños was to cut all rations by 20 percent and to forbid trading with Filipinos for fruit, which was abundant in that area. Among other acts of deliberate cruelty, he took food grown by internees in the camp garden and gave it to the guards, cut the salt ration, and ordered a truck load of fruit left on the asphalt pavement in the tropical sun until it became a truck load of garbage.

Everyone in camp was starving and some were dying. One fellow who got very hungry decided to slip out of the camp and get something to eat. He succeeded, but on his way back the guard caught him and Lt. Konishi ordered a soldier to shoot him. The internee was a Roman Catholic. As he was dying, he wanted a priest, but they wouldn't allow it. After our rescue, Konishi also was responsible for a wholesale massacre of civilians in the town of Los Baños. When the war was over, he was tried and executed for his war crimes.

About that time we were down to about 800 calories a day. A couple of nuns went to the commandant to complain about the short rations, saying that we really were not getting enough to sustain life for very long. Lieutenant Konishi was there. After the nuns had made their plea, he reared back and laughed right in their faces, and said, "Before you get out of here you'll be eating dirt." So here it was, maybe a week later. Paul and I were eating dirt.

At first we had a lot of protein with mongo beans and some meat occasionally. But when all of that was short, we had mostly just rice and a little bit of corn and camp greens. We were quite short on vitamins and a lot of people got Beriberi from lack of Vitamin B. Tempers were running short. About that time a Red Cross shipment arrived. It included some vitamins, especially B1 and B2. The doctors distributed it person by person throughout the camp. It made a big difference.

We did everything we could to supplement our meager rations. Since our buildings were on sloping hills there were terraces on which to put them. We had made a doorway out of our cubicle. On our side of the building there was a flat area extending from the barracks for about eight or 10 feet to a bank. Out on that flat area opposite our cubicles, we set up a little shack with a hibachi type place where we could cook whatever extra food we could find. Almost every family did have some cooking facilities so that if they could get some extra food through the canteen or whatever, they would have a way of dealing with it. Paul scrounged banana peels from the garbage cans and we would fry and eat them. They made a vehicle for the oil and gave us fiber. But, when we ran out of oil, they just dried up like paper. Dr. Blair from Korea, who later died a few days before our rescue, got slugs out of the ditch and fried them. He had to watch them carefully because the slugs didn't want to fry and they would keep crawling out of the pan.

As our rations dwindled to almost nothing, we became very weak. The rainy season was coming. We wanted to make a little walkway from our cubicle, out to the little cooking shed. We laid out a couple of two-by-fours and were putting bamboo slats on them, like a bamboo floor you would have in a nipa house. To do this we had to take some bamboo sections we had gathered and split them. Normally, to split bamboo we would simply take a bolo and hit it right in the middle. In our condition we didn't dare do that because our muscles just weren't reliable. So Paul would take a bolo and lay it down carefully on the end of the bamboo in the middle. Then he would pick up the whole thing and hit the end of the bamboo on the ground. That was working very well for a few shots and then the whole thing would just fly right out of his hands. He wasn't strong enough to hold it.

For our personal firewood we had to cut up pieces of a big old stump on the bank opposite our cubicle. It was filled with some big ants about an inch to an inch-and-a-quarter long. We borrowed a two-man saw and were trying to saw up some of that stump wood. We would rescue a piece from the ants and sit down with it. Then we would pull back and forth on that two-man saw. Maybe we would get in one or two strokes, before one of our hands would just slip right off the handle. We couldn't hold it. We were getting weaker.

Some of the people saved their rice, so as to take a meal in the middle of the night. One little batch (about a large tablespoon full) had spoiled and they didn't dare eat it, so they threw it out. The next barracks was full of women of doubtful character. They got wind of it - that this barracks was throwing away food. Oh what a fuss came up!

Probably the "week of freedom" saved quite a few lives. It came near the end. By then people were dying daily. We were running out of extra tables and benches to use as coffins. It happened this way. Our American troops feinted a landing on the Batangas coast. The main U.S. force, heading for a landing at Lingayen, sailed far enough away from the Philippines so that the few scouting planes the Japanese had left, couldn't spot them easily. At the same time a smaller task force was sent in toward the coast just west of us, as though they were going to make a landing there. So the Japanese started rushing troops south to meet that invasion. The strategy was to draw them south, giving our main force an easier time with the big landing up at Lingayen. That was where the Japanese also had made their first landing. The coolie army of about 80 that guarded our camp decided they didn't want to stay around for the landing. They wanted to get out. They called in the chairman of our Central Committee and handed him the keys to the bodega. They said, "Here, you take care of how much food you want to dole out. We're leaving." And they jumped in their three trucks and took off for Manila.

Our guards left about 3:00 a.m. When we discovered that they were leaving, there was a hurry up scurry to see who had flags for a flag raising ceremony about five o'clock at dawn. Paul borrowed a trumpet and offered to bugle for the flag raising. Someone came up with an American flag, and with a British flag. The Italians didn't have one. By then Italy had surrendered and their citizens were considered enemy aliens. So they had been brought in quite late, compared to the rest of us. The Dutch sisters worked very hard trying to make a Dutch flag, without success. So it was just the American and British flags that were raised.

Early in the morning everyone in the camp gathered together. Paul bugled for that event, and we sang the two national anthems. We raised those two flags and left them up for a while for a little celebration. After that we hauled the flags back down again because we were still in Japanese fighting territory and we didn't want to call attention to this operation. It was for our own benefit. If a Japanese plane had spotted our flags, we would have been an immediate target. Nevertheless some people complained about our taking the flags down.

As we gathered, people asked, "What shall we do?" Some said, "Here's our chance to get away. There are no guards. Let's go!" We argued, "Where are you going? Where can you be safe? Better just stay right here." And that's what we did.

Then our internee guards took over the guard posts around the camp. We manned those guard posts in our usual two hour shifts. Paul was on one of the guard posts from three to five in the morning. Every night in the middle of the night he would get up with the other internee guards and head for the guard post. There were two men at each of the guard posts. Of course they had no firearms, or night sticks or clubs or any weapons of any kind. The only tool they had was whatever persuasion they could offer to anybody who was thinking about leaving. They would make them aware of the fact that we were behind enemy lines. If they were to leave the camp they would have no protection at all. We may not have had much protection within the camp, but it was better than being out there on your own. Reasoning was all they had to work with. A few of the internees did leave, but none through Paul's particular exit.

Before long we raided the storehouse to get food that we could cook for ourselves to add to what we had. I went in with them, and someone put a bag of rice on my back. Down to the ground I went. I just couldn't carry it. I weighed about 110 pounds and I didn't have any strength. People divided up the rice and put it in cans under their beds. But when the Japanese came back we had to return everything we had taken.

During the week of freedom the Central Committee gradually increased the food ration. We immediately went back to two meals a day, but they were small. Not a big increase. We just went back to a low-level two-meal-a-day diet. We gradually increased the rations because we figured that if we were left alone the Filipinos would find a way to get food to us. It was about the third day when some people began to get about all they could handle, considering their shrunken stomachs. Some of the younger fellows were a little better able to handle more food. Three of the young fellows got together and put a sign on the board. "If you can't eat it. See Ken or Len or Paul" They got a few contributions and shared them equally. Everybody was at least having enough to survive, a little more than we had been having. This was a week in January. I do not recall the dates. It was a little more than a month before we were rescued.

Our "Week of Freedom" soon ended. Our captors came back, six days from when they left, practically to the hour. One writer reported that they had been called to Manila to dig trenches. Apparently, when they got to Manila this whole thing had blown over and they had lost a lot of face for leaving. They were sent back. So when they returned, they came with their tails between their legs, so to speak.

When the Japanese returned to the camp Paul and his partner were sitting in the dark in their guard house, with a flood light on at the edge of the camp, shining out in both directions. At 3:00 a.m. they had taken their places and were sitting on two of the three chairs in that little booth. Just about that time, three Japanese trucks rolled in to camp. The first thing those two internee guards knew about it, was when they saws a couple of Japanese soldiers walking down the line. They looked at each other. "They must be back!" Sure enough they were. The two soldiers came down the line, saluted and bowed to the internee guards. They bowed back to the soldiers who then turned and walked on down the line. It was as though the internees were their superior officers. Pretty soon two more soldiers appeared in the dim light in the distance, coming down the path, outside the fence. They ran through the same routine. Apparently they had all been given the same instructions. Each pair of soldiers that came down the path saluted and bowed. Each time the internee guards bowed back and the soldiers turned and walked on down the line. Eventually the first pair of soldiers came back again. Paul recognized them as they got closer. This time the soldiers took their guns down to the ground, bowed again in salute. Once more, the internee guards bowed back. The soldiers looked at each other. Then one of them gestured toward the third chair. The internees nodded and gestured toward the extra chair. So the soldier stepped forward and left his gun with its butt on the ground leaning on the railing right beside Paul. He stepped into the guard house and sat down in the third chair. The other Japanese put his gun along beside the first gun, turned around and sat down on the floor in front of Paul. Paul and his companion looked at each other, glanced over at the guns, grinned at each other, and sat there. After awhile, before the next pair of soldiers came into the light the two Japanese got up, took their guns, bowed again and went off down the line.

Before long, the next pair showed up, much more promptly than before, because the first pair had been sitting there almost until the second pair were due to come. When the second pair arrived, they bowed to the internees, gestured toward the chair, stacked their arms and sat down again. The same routine over and over until the first pair got back again and rested a while. They were apparently gradually taking over. But we didn't abandon our posts until we got word from our organization to do so. Then they took over.

After the return of our captors, the situation got worse. We had to return the rice and other things we had taken after they left us.

One of our missionaries, Dr. McGill had saved about seven cans of meat, under his bed or under his mattress or somewhere. He had been saving them for an emergency. Finally, he got to that stage where he couldn't eat. He was starving and he couldn't use the food he had saved. Four days before our rescue, he died of starvation. I sat by his bed the whole night when he died. He was constantly trying to vomit. There wasn't anything there to come up.

CHAPTER SIX

RESCUE

Viola was very ill with bacillary dysentery. While she was in the camp hospital, we could see the glow of Manila burning. Once again, we anticipated that something was going to happen soon. There were rumors that we were to be executed. When the Japanese dug a big pit, the rumors were reinforced.

On the 17th of February, five days before Washington's Birthday, a lone scout plane, without markings on it, came over, and circled the camp several times. The pilot came low, and buzzed the camp five times. On the fifth time he waggled his wings and left. When Paul reported the incident, he said, "I've been doing some calculation. Five plus seventeen makes 22. February 22 is Washington's Birthday! I wonder if something's going to happen on Washington's birthday."

Two days later that scout plane came over again. This time he buzzed the camp three times. On the third time he waggled his wings and went off, just as he had the first time. Paul said, "Aha, Washington's Birthday! Three days more from the 19th. That must be a signal!"

The day before Washington's birthday, Paul came in and exclaimed, "That plane threw a monkey wrench into the machinery. When he came over today, he didn't just buzz once and waggle his wings. He buzzed twice and waggled his wings." So some of Paul's friends said, "All coincidence. All coincidence! Forget it." But Paul insisted, "Something has gone wrong. They had to change the dates."

As the time drew near, we wondered how we would be rescued. We had heard all kinds of rumors about what kinds of equipment the armed forces had by then. One rumor was that there were tanks that could go under water. Paul said to us, "There may be some kind of vehicle that can go on the water or under the water. So don't be too surprised if our rescue involves a trip across the lake." Viola said, "Paul that's a very deep lake. Those vehicles couldn't go on the bottom of that lake." He said, "Oh mother, don't you read the Popular Mechanics? There are amphibious vehicles that go on land, and then they go on top of the water."

On the morning of February 22, Washington's birthday, Paul was guarding the wood pile by the kitchen, from three to 5:00 a.m. All of a sudden two big groups of P-38s came circling around, away from the camp and over it. The young people were watching them. And some of them got quite excited. One fellow climbed up a tree to get a better look. We were not supposed to watch planes flying over head. The Japanese guards shouted at him to get down. Then, one of them aimed his rifle at the boy. "Better get down from there before you get shot," Paul yelled. That young fellow came down fast when he saw that rifle aimed at him. Paul just stayed on the woodpile and watched. The planes circled around. Then apparently, after one of the passes they must have seen what they were looking for. They formed a single file in a big circle. There were two groups of eleven, 22 of them in all. They started dive bombing. Way off in the distance Paul could see the bombs leaving the planes and disappearing beyond the hill. He began to hear explosions. So he got his stop watch and started timing. From the time the bombs disappeared behind the hill until he heard the explosion was about five or six seconds. Based on the speed of sound he figured it was about 2 kilometers away. Then he noticed that some of the bombs did not seem to explode. A bomb would go down but no sound came. Just as he was about to conclude that the bombs were duds, big columns of black smoke started to rise. He realized then that they were incendiary bombs.

Now Paul had found a reason for the change in dates. "That's why they didn't come today. Maybe tomorrow." He figured there was resistance near our camp that needed to be overcome before our rescue was possible. Later he found out that there probably was a large group of Japanese holed up in caves over there; part of the reserves for the fighting that was going on about 10 miles away. Long after the war, one of the 11th Airborne troopers, who was assigned to work with the guerrillas, told Paul that the planes were part of a buffer.

Sgt. John Fulton (on the left), Radio Operator of the 11th Airborne, with Gordon Watson, a childhood buddy. The banca in this picture is similar to the fishing boat that took Sgt. Fulton across Laguna de Bay, around and behind the Japanese lines. He hid with his radio under the floor boards for several hours while the guerillas, posing as fishermen, evaded Japanese patrol boats.

RESCUE PLAN

Filipino guerillas under Gustav Ingles, studied the routines of the camp guards. Internees, who had escaped from the Los Baños camp, brought additional valuable intelligence. With this and other information, the staff of Major General Joseph Swing developed a rescue plan which worked out something like this.

Several nights before the raid, Filipino guerillas took Sgt. Fulton across Laguna de Bay, behind Japanese lines. He provided radio communication between the guerrillas and the 11th Airborne headquarters. Two nights before the raid, a Reconnaissance Platoon under Lt. George Skau, with twenty Filipino guerrillas, crossed the lake and waited. Early on February 23, just berfore the paratroopers were to jump, they marked the drop zone and prepared to knock out three machine gun pill boxes. At 7:00 a.m. 11th Airborne paratroopers, under John M Ringler, made a low altitude jump. Teams of guerilas, American soldiers and camp escapees eliminated Japanese guards. Fifty-four amtracs of the 672nd Amphibious Battalion arrived. They took 2,147 internees to safety in two trips across the lake. Meanwhile, to the north, troops under Colonel Robert H. Soule engaged the Japanese 8th Tiger Division, serving as a diversionary force and protecting the operation's flank.

Viola was back in our cubicle on sick leave. Later that day she saw another plane flying over us, dragging letters behind it spelling the word "RESCUE." We got very excited, but we didn't know how or when it would happen.

We didn't know it then, but at the time we were to be rescued, the building to building bombardment, fierce room to room and hand to hand combat, for the liberation of Manila was at its height. The desperate battle line of resistance from Japanese troops had intersected the huge Laguna de Bay lake, south of Manila, not far from our Los Baños camp. A couple of Internees had been in and out of camp several times, and had made contact with Filipino guerillas. Together, they had carefully studied the daily routine of our captors and their defenses. Several times they had crossed the lake at night, around Japanese lines, and had succeeded in getting word to General MacArthur that we were about to be executed. They had given all their detailed information to those who were planning our liberation.

In order to save our lives, MacArthur took the 11th Airborne paratroopers off the lines in the fierce battle of Manila. And in one of the most miraculous rescues of the entire war, the attack had been meticulously planned, and was flawlessly executed by guerillas, paratroopers and amphibious tractors. There were no casualties among the 2,147 internees, including a three-day-old baby girl. However, two paratroopers and two guerillas had been killed, and there were casualties in the diversionary force attacking the Japanese lines.

The next day, February 23, 1945, was a wonderful exciting time. Early in the morning, about an hour before light, we heard a funny rumbling noise and we couldn't guess just what it would be. Later we learned it was from fifty four amtracs of the 672nd Amphibious Battalion, coming to take us to safety across Laguna de Bay. They had made the long overland trip from Cabanatuan, then across the huge lake, around the Japanese lines , and finally two miles overland to our camp.

For those who want more details, an excellent summary of the "Raid at Los Baños" can be read on the internet, in the Wikipedia free encyclopedia report, or can be seen on the outstanding History Channel documentary called "Rescue at Dawn."

The morning of our rescue, the bell rang for us to assemble for roll call. Every morning at seven we assembled. I was a monitor of the barracks and had to be sure to report on any who were ill. Sometimes I was late in getting there. They understood that. All the rest had to assemble to report. Some days there would be two or three who would remain in the barracks because of illness. This morning the bell rang, and I started to shout "roll call." The planes flew overhead and the paratroopers bailed out just as the bell rang so nobody went out for roll call. Our Japanese guards were raw recruits and they had no way to shoot at those planes. The rescue had begun.

Later we learned that the hour of 7:00 a.m. had been chosen for the attack because, at that hour, the Japanese soldiers had stacked their rifles and were engaged in their morning calisthenics. The attackers reached the rifles before the Japanese could get there.

There was a sharp exchange of shots. Everybody got down on the floor under the beds and waited. Firing went on for a few minutes and we stayed under the beds. Only two of the internees were hit. One of them had a bullet go across her abdomen, but it didn't penetrate.

As had been previously arranged, the guerrillas, had surrounded the camp and engaged the guards, killing many of them. The paratroopers landed and there was a skirmish between them and some of the guards. Our guards there at the camp were very green recruits. They weren't combat troops. They were untrained, and were not very efficient. So when the paratroopers came to take us out of the camp, the guards who had not been killed fled, and went into hiding.

There was quite an excitement as the Americans came through the barracks. Suddenly, in the midst of the firing, an American soldier came through our barracks shouting, "Any Nips in here? Any Nips in here?" Just at that moment an internee, who was eagerly waiting to see an American soldier, saw the paratrooper and cried, "There's one!" Whirling around with his gun at the ready, the soldier shouted back, "Where? Where is he?"

Meanwhile, Paul had been having an exciting time of his own. He had been guarding the camp gardens that morning from three to five. At five o'clock he got back into bed. He was supposed to sleep in, because he had permission not to show up at seven o'clock roll call. I'll let him tell his own story here.

I was in the sack and I heard someone call out, "Parachutes!" I bounced about once on the ladder on the way down to the cubicle floor, and went out the side door and looked. Sure enough the sky was full of parachutes with what looked like coffins hanging under them. I didn't see any movement or anything. Some of them may have been boxes of arms and ammunition. Apparently the rescue was on the way.

I went back in and grabbed my yellow arm band, which indicated I was an internee guard. As I was throwing that on I ran down the aisle to the cubicle where my internee guard captain lived. "What's my assignment?" I shouted. I don't know how much of a plan he had worked out ahead of time. But he said, "Go over next door and out the back and tell the people in barracks 26 and 27 to stay out of the way."

I got up to the point where I could see the Japanese guard who was in the one man guard post about half way down the back line. He was standing there, looking around, wondering what was going to happen next. I knew I didn't have time to get to those two barracks. At least that was my intuition. So I stayed out of that guard's line of sight but in view of the two barracks. I just cupped my hands and shouted at them back and forth, first to one and then to the other. They were gathering out in front for their roll call. "Get back inside!" I shouted. I kept yelling at them until they got the message and started disappearing.

About that time I looked at the guard again. Then all of a sudden, all hell broke loose. That was when the guerrillas opened up on the guards who were around the camp perimeter, and attacked the guards that were doing their setting-up exercises. They were throwing grenades in where the Japanese gun racks were, to mess

59

that up. The guerrillas opened the battle. Each had particular guards assigned them and they all attacked simultaneously. The paratroopers followed. It was amazingly well timed.

I went back into the barracks I had come through. Back of it was an auxiliary hospital. I told the patients there, "Just stay in bed. Don't try to move around. You have just as good a chance there as anywhere." Then I went back to the middle of the barracks and shouted to the front part which was a men's barracks. "Everybody hit the deck," I screamed. And I set a good example in the aisle. There were one or two that had to stick their heads out the window. One guy just about got shot doing it. Bullets started whizzing around. I had always thought all those sound effects in Western movies, with singing bullets, and all that stuff, was partly a put-up job. But it's very real. That's the way it is. When a bullet hits something, it sings.

After a while the shooting died down. We started getting up. I said to the fellows, as I walked to the front of the barracks, "Now remember, if it starts up again, you know what to do. Hit the deck and stay out of the way. No use getting hurt."

I decided to go into the next barracks to see how they were doing. I had to cross some space, and a road and some more space down a path to get there. I got ready to shove off. I put a hand on either side of the front door jam. I tensed my muscles, and was about to catapult forward. Then, BANG! It all went off again. Again I cried, `Hit the deck!' I turned around and went down. And so did everybody else.

When it subsided again, here came this fellow I knew from the internee guard group. As he came through, he shouted, "Spread the word the best you can. Just grab what you can carry and let's get out of here. They're going to burn the whole place down." So I headed back the road to the other barracks and spread the word. I got back to our barracks and told them; went back to my cubicle and grabbed what I could, and headed for the door.

It was not long before the shooting was over. Soon the order came to leave the barracks and be ready to be taken away. We were told not to take any baggage, but just a few personal things that we needed.

The amtracs came up near the barracks. The soldiers loaded as many of the internees as they could into the amtracs and started back toward the lake. The rest of us were told to walk down to the shore where they would come back for us.

Paul put on a couple of extra layers of clothing, because he didn't know they were going to give us some nice new olive drabs when we got out. He was wearing about three layers of clothing. Viola did the same. Paul grabbed his Bible, his New Testament and his tool box with a bunch of heavy tools and off he went, walking down toward the gate.

I waited to be sure that everybody was evacuated, and that all my barracks were clear. Viola waited with me. We were the last to leave. When they were all clear, we started walking toward the lake. It would be an hour before those amtracs could go across the lake and come back for us.

Before we had gotten 50 yards from the buildings, we turned back and saw our barracks in flames. It was a bamboo barracks and it wouldn't take much to set that whole thing on fire. Our men themselves had set fire to the buildings, so they wouldn't be a haven for the Japanese later. I went back a month later and found a little metal trinket that had been melted by the heat of that flame.

I had a little package of some very valuable mission papers, including a code book with my record of those financial transactions with the Chinese merchants. But, I saw one woman struggling to carry a little suitcase which was very precious to her. She couldn't handle it. A lot of us didn't have very much strength either. My bag of papers was much lighter. So I said to her, "Let me carry your suitcase. And you take this little package of papers that I want to save. It's not very heavy."

When we got about a quarter of a mile away from the camp, I discovered that she didn't have the package with her. She had forgotten it in the excitement. At that point, I should have forgotten it, and just left it there. They were valuable papers, but not as valuable as our lives, of course. But I decided to go back and get it. "Oh, she said, I left it at the place where we were waiting."

There were no Japanese in sight. So I went back to get my package, and found it exactly where I had left it. She hadn't even picked it up. My path went back right along the side of a ravine. In fact, the package had been put down right there. I didn't realize, at the time, that the Japanese who survived the attack, were all hiding down in that ravine. Fortunately, they were too excited, or too scared to do anything. The guards from the camp of course, were thoroughly cowed for the time being. They were inexperienced and I don't think they had their heart in it at all.

When I turned back for that package, I had almost caught up with Paul. As I started back, he turned around and came toward me to find out what was the matter. But one of the rescuers said, "No! Don't go back! He'll be O.K."

Before I left her, Viola was picked up by an army doctor in a jeep. He had come up to the camp with a jeep and a trailer to help with anyone who was sick or needed special help. Paul had been stumbling along with his heavy tool box. So the doctor told him to put his things in the trailer.

Viola rode on down to the shore. She had some garments she wanted to save, if and when we got to the States. On a hot summer day she had put on a big coat with a fur collar. She wanted to save that because it just might be cold. She was rigged out with all those clothes she was trying to save. It was really something to see her sitting up on top of the hood of that jeep like a queen in a procession, I guess. And that was the last I saw of her until we got to the shore where the amtracs came back for us.

On her way down to the shore Viola had quite an exciting skirmish. A Japanese sniper attacked them, so they got out and hid behind a building. Paul, who was following some distance back, heard the sniper fire and jumped off the side of the road. He ducked under a small nipa house along with several others and waited until the firing stopped. Then they got back on the road and headed down to the lake.

I got the package, and walked all the way down to the crossroads, about a quarter of a mile. We stopped at that crossroads for a few moments where some internees were resting. There was no more transportation down to the waterfront. The houses were pretty well vacant. Almost everybody had left. But I tried to get some Filipinos, who were there, to find some food for us, any food that was left, cold camotes, or anything. There was a Roman Catholic priest there. He had two or three cans of food that he had saved from his stuff. I've forgotten now what I had to trade. At any rate, we traded with people at the crossroads so we got a little better food than we had in the camp.

A Filipino gave Paul a banana and someone gave me a coconut. At the shore, we opened the coconut and shared it. The rear guard stayed on the beach with three amtracs. The other amtracs came back and loaded up group after group. Probably, each of them made at least two trips, except for that rear guard group.

We were standing there waiting and eating our coconut. All the time we were waiting for the amtracs, shells were bursting in the water and landing on the beach off to our left about a couple of hundred yards. We thought it was an attack, that maybe the Japanese were firing at us. But later we learned that our own forces were providing a protective screen to prevent the Japanese from attacking us.

Some of the P-38s were circling overhead. But instead of circling over us, they were circling over the area of the empty beach. All the time they were keeping an eye on us but drawing the enemy fire elsewhere. The Japanese troops were shelling the area under the planes.

As we were waiting, Paul saw some amtracs stuck in the middle of the lake. He picked up his tools from the jeep and started talking to one of the rear guard group. The soldier said, "I'm supposed to go and work on some of those amtracs out there, to get them going again and we don't have enough tools." "Well you take these then," Paul offered.

The soldier accepted Paul's tools, and that was the last he saw of them. So what Paul had left, besides his three layers of clothes, was his Bible and New Testament. Later, Paul met a Jewish lad who was in the field hospital which was also quartered at Montinlupa. When Paul found that his new friend wanted a copy of the scriptures, Paul gave him his Bible. So Paul came out with only his New Testament.

We were in the last group of internees to be picked up. The rear guard group came after us. Later, we learned that the P-38s had told the commanders of the operation that they could hold off the Japanese and maintain an open corridor to the lake for seven hours. Paul looked at his watch as we boarded the last amtrack. It was five minutes after two, almost exactly seven hours since the operation began at seven in the morning.

While we were crossing the lake there were shells and bullets passing over us, and we had to keep down below the edge of the amtracs. When we were out in the middle of the lake, Paul nudged Viola and said, "Mother, didn't I tell you we might get rescued across the lake?"

It was quite a stirring day.

On the other side of the lake, the amtracs took us ashore. As we debarked, some of the welcoming Filipinos on shore gave us rice wrapped in coconut leaves. Oh, but that tasted good! Trucks and jeeps were waiting to take us to Montinlupa, the Insular Prison. The Americans had already occupied it and released the political prisoners that had been jailed there. We boarded the vehicles. As we went through the villages on the way to Montinlupa, people were holding up the "V" for victory sign and shouting welcome.

The Smith family is shown here just after they arrived at the safety of Montinlupa Insular Prison. The U.S. Army was using it as a temporary haven for the rescued internees. From right to left, Stephen L. Smith, Viola Smith, Paul L. Smith, and two unidentified internee children.

When we got to Montinlupa, they sat us down to feed us. They gave us a cup of soup. It was much more nourishing soup than we had in the camp. Of course, some of us already had food from the Filipinos along the way. Our hosts were trying to be very careful because two people in Santo Tomas had died of overeating when they were rescued. So they were being very careful about how much they gave us. Besides this bowl of soup they gave us each two K-Ration bars with a very heavy warning, "This is very rich chocolate," they cautioned. "Don't go gobbling them down. That will get you in trouble. Eat them very slowly and eat only one, tonight. Save the other for morning." They gave us each three packs of cigarettes so that anyone who wanted to smoke could do so.

The prison had just been evacuated, and I don't know just how much they had done to clean it up, bedbugs or whatever. But we were so happy to be there, we weren't troubled about that. The sleeping situation was a little difficult. I had to fix a comfortable bed for Viola who was very thin. I weighed about 110 pounds and she was near 95. I wanted to give her a comfortable place to sleep.

So I used one of the blankets that was available, instead of the boards in the prison bunk, to fix her a better place. We took the boards out and took blankets and fastened them on either side so they made a softer bed than the board bunks that the prisoners had used. I can't remember where I slept.

Early in our stay at Montinlupa we could hear the sounds of battle around us and in the distance. The big guns were still booming. The Japanese were still occupying some of the area near Montinlupa. The situation was tense.

The enemy came up to the prison one day and all our guns went off. We were in line for a meal and we had to run for the barracks. Viola, who was in a woman's barracks was terribly frightened. She thought, "Oh my, here we are free, and now they're going to get us anyway. Maybe I won't see Stephen and Paul again."

Along toward the end of our stay at Montinlupa, a Filipino came to see me. The guards called me, and I went to the gate to visit with him. I don't think they were letting any Filipinos in at that point. As I was visiting with him, a sniper almost got me. The bullet practically singed my ear. There was a lot of excitement. And there was quite a scramble trying to find this sniper who was right in that area. I don't know if they found him or not. So it was not exactly a free situation. However, we did have a good high wall around the prison which protected us from snipers.

They kept us in Montinlupa for about six weeks as a temporary refuge until we could be taken back to the States, and also to bring us back to normal in our feeding. We were skin and bones, and joked about that. We said, "There are only two diseases we could possibly get now. Skin disease and bone disease."

We lined up for food three times a day. And while we were waiting we would sit down. The line would move and we would sit down again. Some people who got in the food line earliest went through, sat down, and then got back in line again. But our hosts finally caught onto that.

I tried once or twice to get to the end of the line and go through again. But it didn't work too well.

At first, our food was flown in to us and dumped by parachute. They were fighting between us and Manila. A package of powdered eggs fell out of the chute and burst open. They gave Paul a can and he began eating it dry right out of the can. We would put it in a cup, with water and stir it, and eat it. It was so good! Yet it was too much for us. Paul and Viola both got terrible sores in their mouths.

The troops used a lot of canned goods. In the dump we got big cans, and with the scrap iron we found there, we made handles for them so we could get a good big cup full of coffee.

As soon as I could, I got a pass and went into Manila to see how things were and what had happened to our Mission property. I got a ride in a military jeep, then rode on a horse drawn carratela. I stayed all night with a Filipino friend who was a doctor. I forget his name now. It was fortunate he was a doctor, because I had bought some peanuts from a vendor that day. I love peanuts. And being as hungry as I was, I ate too many of them, and didn't chew them very well. I was about as sick then, as I have ever been. It was too much for my digestive tract. I shouldn't have taken it. But the doctor knew what to do.

The battle of Manila destroyed all our houses. There was a little bit of roof left and some posts. It was a real mess, very soon after the fighting. Buoys from the bay had been dragged up there to be used as barricades. Going back there was quite an unforgettable experience.

Somehow I got a hold of a bicycle and rode down town. Army engineers had put up a Bailey bridge along a side of the old Jones bridge which had been destroyed. I carried the bicycle across. On the other side, I looked down the Escolta, the former "Fifth Avenue" of Manila. It was just one big mess. The buildings were so destroyed we could hardly look down the street.

After about six weeks in Montinlupa, we were brought home to the States to recuperate. We boarded the Eberly, a new troop transport ship that was not properly ballasted. In one storm we almost capsized. We were with escort ships for protection until we got out of Philippine waters. But the Eberly was capable of about 18 knots an hour, so we just took off on our own. We arrived in Los Angeles. Home at Last!

For several weeks after our return to the States, Viola and I gained two pounds a day. We needed time to recover.

CHAPTER SEVEN

OUT OF THE RUBBLE AND INTO ETERNITY

We survived war's crucible!   Before the war, my first career in the isolated forests, mountains and nearby islands of southern Luzon had ended. My second career, in nurturing and empowering a vital national church, had just begun.

I needed to return to Manila. Destruction of church related property was extensive. The war had taken a heavy toll on the church and its leadership. Heavy administrative responsibilities rested on my shoulders. There was too much work waiting to be done and no one there to do it.

After several months of recuperation and without my full year of furlough, I returned to the Philippines, sailing into Manila bay on February 23, 1946. That was the exact first anniversary of our rescue from the Los Baños internment camp. About six months later Viola followed.

Paul remained in California to study.

Recovery

The Japanese Religious Section had forced different Christian churches into one united organization in order to keep control of their activities. This had disrupted all normal ecclesiastical functions. In 1940, before the war, I had been General Secretary of the United Evangelical Church. No one had been selected to succeed me. Everything was at a stand still. I had to get that organization going.

At the same time I was Executive Secretary of the Presbyterian Mission, and needed to get ready for a delegation from our Board of Foreign Missions. It was coming in two or three months to visit our mission areas and study our situation. There was much to do before they arrived.

As soon as possible after war's end, and after a time of recovery, Stephen Smith returned to Manila. He was needed there to help restart church-related programs and to initiate reconstruction of church owned buildings throughout the Philippines. This ruined hospital in Albay, was where his two younger sons had been born.

Immediately after the war, when the banks were open again, we were able to redeem the drafts that we sold during the war.

I was on the Board of Trustees of six different schools: Union Theological Seminary, Silliman University, the Philippine Christian Colleges, Union High School of Manila, Bethel Girls School, and the Christian School in Albay.

The Board of Trustees of the Union Theological Seminary was no longer functioning. Several of the trustees got together in the Manila Hotel to decide what to do. There was the Methodist Bishop of that jurisdiction, several others from our United Evangelical Church and all of those concerned with the seminary. The Bishop then practically appointed me President of the Board of Trustees of the Seminary. That is, he suggested it and our people agreed. I took over as President of the Board of Trustees, the last American to serve in that capacity.

Reconstruction

In order to open the seminary, we had to reconstruct its three story building. The Japanese had made it into a communication center. In one of the large rooms down stairs they had installed a huge piece of equipment with tremendous cement foundations. One big job was getting that very heavy machinery out. We also had to organize a faculty.

Some say, that next to Warsaw, Manila was the most badly damaged city of the war. We needed to reconstruct many buildings in and around Manila. The Ellinwood Girls School had to be rebuilt. The floors and other building materials had been looted. All the residences we had before the war had been destroyed. After the fighting, the U.S. Army had simply bulldozed the rubble off large sections of the city in that area. We built three new residences. The Union High School building was a shambles. Part of it had to be taken down and rebuilt.

Throughout the Philippines 150 church buildings had been destroyed. There was a great need for financial assistance as these congregations sought to rebuild. Our Presbyterian Church raised money through a Restoration Fund. Meanwhile, driven by the Spirit's urge, many of those congregations went to work before any assistance could be provided. Burdened almost beyond their strength, they rebuilt their houses of worship without waiting for financial assistance. The Church as a whole was truly alive and was not waiting for outside help.

The chapel at Silliman University was awaiting completion. I was Vice-Chairman of the Board of Trustees there, and that demanded my attention.

The property in the different mission stations had to be checked. In Legaspi, the Milwaukee Hospital building was thoroughly destroyed. Kenneth MacDonald took responsibility for rebuilding that, and for reconstructing the Church building across from the Hospital.

During this reconstruction period there was too much to do for too few people. Somehow, one had to be in the right place at the right time, and that was impossible. In the kaleidoscope of conflicting demands much that should have been done was overlooked. I can hardly remember everything I had to do. I don't think I preached more than two or three times during that first year after the war, a real deprivation for me.

After those first few hectic months I was relieved of my responsibilities as Executive Secretary of the Mission. The Presbyterian Board of Foreign Missions was intent on giving full control of its mission work to the national church. The Mission, as an organization of American missionaries, was disbanded. Missionaries became "fraternal workers," and the Philippine Church assumed full responsibility for their work. The United Evangelical Church included work that had been started by the Disciples of Christ, the United Brethren, the Congregational and the Presbyterian Churches. An Interboard Representative came out to serve as liaison between those denominations and the Philippine church.

Renewal

Those changes allowed me to concentrate attention on my responsibilities as Executive Secretary of the United Evangelical Church. My great joy during that period was to experience the growing vitality of that Church which had suffered so much during the war. As never before there was a sense of its oneness across all boundaries. I found a deepening desire in many hearts for genuine faith in Christ. There was a widespread conviction of the basic unity of all believers and a passionate desire for organized church union.

In 1958, when the United Evangelical Church became a part of the new United Church of Christ in the Philippines (U.C.C.P.) I became its first General Secretary. For four years till 1962, I was responsible for coordinating the work of the whole denomination.

Upon return from furlough, in August 1951, I focused on accelerating the nationalization of church leadership. In May 1952 Bishop Leonardo Dia replaced me as General Secretary. It organized the Philippine

Board of Missions. The following year I became its Executive Secretary, serving in that capacity until my retirement in June 1962,

That Mission Board was responsible for work among tribal people in the Mountain Province in northern Luzon and among the Bilaans, a hunting and fishing tribe in the mountains of Mindanao. The Bilaans were almost as primitive as the Tsadays that have had so much attention in recent years.

In 1958, after 12 years of work among the Bilaans, approximately a thousand adults had been baptized and five hundred children under the age of 12. Three full time Filipino missionaries, wholly supported by the Philippine church were living among them. Miss Socorro Ayala conducted a medical clinic, and Rev. and Mrs. Lorenzo Genotiva worked in strengthening the church there.

During my tenure, the U.C.C.P. sent 31 Filipino missionaries to about 10 different countries: to Thailand, Indonesia, Malaya, Iran, Ethiopia, Greece, Turkey, Korea, Egypt, and the United States. Among them were teachers, nurses, a theological professor and other ministers. Some of those who had served as missionaries later became many of the strong leaders of the United Church of Christ in the Philippines.

This ecumenical outreach gave the Church a different idea of the presence of American workers in their midst. They realized that it wasn't a Christian America sending to a heathen Philippines. It was Christians in the Church in America helping the Filipinos meet their responsibility in the Philippines. And it was Christians in the Philippines helping the American church meet its challenge in the United States.

The Philippine church could not afford large sums of money for this work. The cooperating Mission Boards in America put up the major part. The Philippine share in the support of these missionaries was almost a token amount, perhaps 25%.

Again and again we saw churches revitalized as they caught the vision of their missionary responsibility. That was the most satisfying service that was permitted me in all my forty-two years in the Philippines.

A Blossoming Music Ministry

After the war, Viola's budding Philippine career in church music opened into full bloom. She was instrumental in bringing together a faculty of outstanding Filipina musicians and organizing a College of Sacred Music in Manila. This later became a department in the Seminary.

In February 1947 she directed a Festival of Sacred Music with 382 voices from various denominations in Manila. A summer choir school, directed by Flora Zarco, followed shortly thereafter with 129 students of seven denominations from nine provinces.

For several years Viola wrote and produced a half hour radio program of live sacred music. In 1953, she organized a twenty-five-member Choirmasters guild which sponsored a Festival Choir of two hundred voices from twenty-eight congregations in eleven denominations. Viola was chosen as the director. The choir gave two regular concerts a year. They sang at the Easter sunrise service for the Philippine Federation of Christian Churches and at a Bataan Day Memorial Service on the Luneta. For the Billy Graham Crusade in 1956 the Festival Choir was enlarged to a choir of one thousand with Cliff Barrows and Viola sharing in conducting it.

All these musical accomplishments were significant. But Viola's greatest contribution was to the lives of her pupils and colleagues, who have made significant contributions to the music of the churches in the Philippines.

Retirement

In June 1962, 42 years after we began our work there, we left our beloved Philippines for the last time. My second career as a Church Administrator had come to a close.

We made our retirement home in Watsonville, California where Viola had lived as a young woman. It was there that my third career began. Twice during the next 20 years I served the Presbyterian Church there as Interim Pastor. Between those terms I was their Associate Pastor.

When I finally did retire again, they made me Pastor Emeritus.   That meant a great deal to me.

My life is drawing to a close.   It has been nearly ninety years now. Memories search those years for the meaning of it all.   And I find it in God's Hands.   There have been many times when I did not realize it. Yet, looking back, I know that even before I could possibly have been conscious of a loving God, I was in those guiding and loving hands.

When my time comes, I will be in God's Hands just as, in life, I have been in God's hands. Join me then in gratitude to God, for memory and for the inspiration of the Holy Spirit, who leads us in paths that we do not know.   And that really is my story.

The Rev Dr. Stephen L. Smith went to be with his Lord on July 7, 1983 in Duarte California.

From 1920 to 1939, home for the Stephen L. Smith family was at the foot of the beautiful and powerful Mayon Volcano. Awesome eruptions in 1928 and 1938 sent huge lava flows down the side of the mountain almost into the sea. Smoke rose from the crater five miles into the air. Every two or three hours the mountain roared like a deranged giant. Several times, for a whole hour, deep thunderous rumbles sounded like Niagara Falls.

MY FIRST CAREER IN ISOLATED RURAL PHILIPPINES

In 1920, no one could doubt that we had been given an isolated rural assignment. It had taken our ship a day and a half to make the trip from Manila on the west coast of Luzon, through the treacherous San Bernardino Straights at the southern tip of Luzon to Legaspi on the east coast of the island. There was no other way to get there in those days. It was so remote that for several years after that, we got our mail about every week or ten days, and not always then. In later years, when the train finally got through to us, we went to Manila first by train, then by a small overnight boat trip, then by bus, and finally by train again. Today it is a short plane trip away.

Legaspi port was like nothing we had ever seen. It was located at the foot of Mayon Volcano, arguably the most beautiful perfect cone in the world, rising eight thousand feet right out of the sea. The beach of black volcanic sand drops very steeply into deep water. The piers had to be rather short, and ships could not tie up along side them. A ship would back up with its stern to the dock. A long wooden gang plank set at a steep angle from the stern to the pier provided the path for loading and unloading the ship. We had to go down that plank without any railing. It did have some cleats to keep us from slipping into the sea. We made it all right, and our baggage followed us. But I wouldn't want to do that now!

Twentieth Century Tongues

We had been sent to the Bicol region to work closely with people in rural homes and small villages. It is impossible to cross cultural boundaries without understanding the language of the people. My first assignment was to learn their language.

Contrary to what most people think, Spanish is not used extensively in the Philippines.

However, since the Philippines had been a Spanish colony prior to the Spanish American War, I suspect that one reason our Mission Board had thought of us for the Philippines, was because of my extensive prior study of Spanish.

In the Philippines there are eight languages and 63 dialects, distinct enough to be separate one from the other. The Bicol language, which is spoken where we would be working, in Southern Luzon, is one of the Malay dialects. It would be my principal tool for the next 19 years.

I was given the wonderful opportunity of spending almost my full time for two years in learning that language. I had also been assigned responsibility for the high school boy's dormitory. It gave me a chance to practice the language I was learning, and provided a meaningful diversion from the rigorous demands of language study. Since the boys were having all their classes in English, it was possible to minister to them in meaningful ways. My other assignment was to conduct English language services every Sunday evening. We lived in an apartment on the second floor of the dormitory, and our two younger sons were born there.

I devoted my time to studying the language. With a lot of cards I made a Bicol dictionary for myself. I took a Bicol New Testament and pasted it in one column of print on a large page. In the margins I wrote a number of grammatical notes. Without realizing it at the time, I was thereby preparing myself for revising the Bicol translation of the New Testament.

In the beginning of his "First Career" Stephen L. Smith (left), spent two years mastering the Bicol. language. He then joined four others to revise the Bicol translation of the New Testament for the American Bible Society.

Translating the New Testament

In our third year, when I was well along in my language study, the American Bible Society decided we needed a new translation of the Bicol New Testament. The printing plates for the Bicol Bible were destroyed in the great Japanese earthquake of 1923. And it was the policy of the Bible Society to revise their translations under such circumstances

The Bicol New Testament we were using had been translated by a Spanish pharmacist, who had married in the area and had lived there a good many years. He had picked up some Bicol. But it was his second language. He worked without the benefit of Filipino colleagues who knew the language. Working from a Spanish New Testament, he had done the best he could. His Spanish grammar colored his translation. There were so many errors in the use of Bicol that a new translation was desperately needed.

In 1923, a committee of three Filipinos and two Americans, started to retranslate the New Testament into the Bicol tongue. Agripina Moralde, one of our Bible Women who became the first ordained woman in the Bicol region, was a key member of the committee along with two other Filipino pastors. With my study of Greek and of Bicol I was ready to tackle the job. Kenneth MacDonald and I completed the committee of five.

Translation was pretty much a full time job for the committee from 1923 to 1925. We worked five hours a day. This task really consolidated and refined my knowledge of the Bicol language. The differences of opinion on this and that brought out nuances of meaning that wouldn't have been possible under ordinary circumstances.

There were so many glaring mistakes in the old translation that our committee had to develop what was almost a completely new translation.

We made as many as twenty or thirty corrections on every page. An example will illustrate our problem.

We came upon one very funny mistake. Paul's exhortation "Husbands love your wives," in Ephesians 5:25, had come, in the evolution of spoken Bicol, to mean "Husbands fool your wives." How did that happen? Bicol, like all other Philippine languages is very polite. There are no imperatives. They would not express Paul's thought in the imperative form: "Husbands love your wives." Rather they would put it in the passive. So it would be translated "Husbands let your wives be loved by you."

A language in its growth picks up words from other languages. Among the Spanish nouns that Bicol uses is "Camote," the Spanish word for sweet potato. Pagkamaot is the Bicol noun for love. And, it happens that in Bicol, "camote" is also the imperative form for the verb "to love." In Bicol slang "camote" had come to mean "to fool someone." So when Paul's words were translated in the direct imperative they really said "Husbands, fool your wives." People just couldn't understand that. We had to change it. The mistake came when a foreigner, working without Filipino colleagues used the imperative when he should have used the passive.

Since Bicol does not use a direct imperative at all, the remedy was much more far reaching than correcting that one example. It was necessary to change the imperative to the passive form all the way through the New Testament.

It was the practice of many mission organizations at that time, to have their missionaries take a one year furlough after five years service. The furlough was used for study, promotional work in the churches, for rest and renewal, and to reestablish contact with family and friends.

Before leaving on furlough our committee had completed everything except the book of Revelation. Maybe ninety percent of the translation was finished before I left. The rest was completed while I was on furlough. But the experience of working that out really laid a good foundation for my later work in the Bicol language. It has been forty years since I have used Bicol. But I think that even now I could probably preach a sermon in it.

Through Jungles, Over Mountains, and Rivers, and Seas

From 1926 to 1939 I spent most of my time traveling throughout the southern Luzon and neighboring islands, engaged mostly in evangelism, Bible teaching, strengthening congregations and developing the leadership of the churches.

Doctor and Mrs. William McAnlis had come. The large reinforced concrete building, in which we had lived during our first term, had been converted into a hospital. A couple of able young Filipino doctors had joined him on the staff there. That hospital became noted throughout the region for the quality of its care.

For a number of years the heaviest part of the field work fell to me. I traveled all over the region, spending a week or two in each place. At first, Kenneth MacDonald and I used to go together. Later, when I had become acquainted I went on my own, often with Filipino colleagues. Kenneth was increasingly engaged in supervising the construction of several reinforced concrete buildings: a beautiful new church building across from the hospital, a Student Center near the government school campus, and several missionary residences. He also managed our print shop. In one of its busy years our small press printed 1,548,135 pages of literature, and turned out 206,517 pages of mimeographed material. A church paper in Bicol brought our congregations local and general church news. There was an editorial on a vital Christian topic, and a discussion of topics for the Christian Endeavor groups that were active throughout our region.

We placed a very heavy emphasis on distribution of the Word of God. In one busy year more than 18,000 Bibles, New Testaments and portions of Scripture were sold and distributed, while nearly 60,000 pages of Scriptural tracts were given away.

The Bicol area is made up of four provinces and one sub-province. One and a quarter million people speak the Bicol tongue. I was out in the provinces, away from home more than half the time. All of our preaching and teaching was in Bicol. Sometimes I would be gone a week, sometimes two or three weeks.

In the early days, we had Bible classes during the day and evangelistic meetings in the evenings. Meetings were often held out in the plaza, just informal gatherings. We didn't even have to have a formal permit. We just set up the organ and started. Often I would be playing the little portable Este pump organ, and sometimes my cornet.

We would usually stay a week or ten days in one place. Sometimes we were starting new groups in remote places without previous church connections. But often it was an extension of a local congregation. Part of the reason for an extended stay was to give instruction to those who had professed their faith, before we baptized them.

We decided where we would go largely in response to some indication of receptivity. If we got word that there was somebody interested, we would follow up and go into that area. In the early days before the church was well established, we took the initiative in deciding where to go. Later however, as the church began to grow, we changed our emphasis and followed the guidance of the Filipino church leaders. That was a very important development, since from the very beginning our goal had been to establish churches that would be self-governing, self-supporting, and self- propagating.

We made several trips to the island of Catanduanes, and usually stayed for a number of weeks, because of the difficulty of travel there. We moved from one barrio to another by invitation. Someone who had attended a meeting of ours in one place would invite us to the next place and then guide us there. We had plenty of invitations. We would work out from one area to a neighboring area. And people there would invite their friends to our meetings, and so on.

As we traveled, we had very primitive situations to deal with. Sometimes I would sleep on a dining table five feet long. Not very comfortable for a six footer like myself. So after a while I developed a system for my sleeping comfort.

I had a canvas strip made about the width of a cot, and long enough for sleeping. Then a carpenter fashioned two sticks of camagone wood, as strong as steel. These were attached at each end of the canvas so I could roll it up and carry it with me as a hammock.

Houses in the rural areas of the Philippines are built around posts stuck in the ground. These houses, with thatched roofs and walls, are usually small enough to have four posts, one in each corner and the posts are about two and a half feet from the wall in the corner. The posts are about one foot or more in diameter and are of very hard wood that the termites wouldn't eat. The framework of the house, made of bamboo, is tied onto these posts with rattan.

I would string my hammock between two corner posts at the side of the room and out of the way. It was stretched tight by hanging it about six feet up with one set of ropes at each end. Then I would eliminate the sagging by pulling down with another set of ropes at each end so that it was stretched taut and was almost as flat and stable as a bed. It made a very comfortable bed and didn't take long to set up. I left it tight during the day with the bedding folded on it. Then when we moved, the hammock could be rolled up for transport.

At the beginning, I had trouble getting used to the food. We ate camotes (our name for sweet potatoes) and rice and fish and the various dishes that they prepared. I liked rice and of course, could always eat that. But I couldn't always eat the mixtures they had with the rice. Under the right circumstances, I might let them know what I didn't care for.

The eggs they served me were not always as fresh as they might be. For breakfast they would usually cook the eggs very early in the morning long before we ate them. They were stone cold when we got to them.

We did carry some food with us to supplement what we got, such as canned corned beef, evaporated milk, and soup. But in general we ate what was provided.

The Filipino people are extravagantly hospitable. Most of the folk with whom I stayed were very poor. In spite of that, when they discovered what I liked to eat they would go to great lengths to provide it. I always had enough to eat. But I was always glad to get home to familiar food.

Over the last 13 years of his "First Career," Stephen Smith climbed mountains and forded countless streams as he served rural churches in the Bicol. region of Southern Luzon and neighboring islands.

We traveled by every kind of transportation you can imagine. I traveled a lot by bus, and occasionally by train. When we were going to a place near the road, we often went by car. But if we had to go inland from the road, we went by bus, and then by carabao back, or horseback. I didn't often ride a carabao. They are too wide of beam, a very difficult animal to ride. You can't straddle them. You can't curl your legs around them to help you stay aboard. And, we often had to go through very deep mud.

Hiking was most common. We walked for miles and miles in the mountains. When we went back into some of the most remote areas, we had cargadores carrying some of our stuff. My love for hiking in the hills around Los Angeles was good preparation for this.

On rivers we took large bancas carved out of tree trunks.

There are seven thousand islands in the Philippines. An island is anything that is out of the water at high tide. But, I suppose, there are no more than several hundred occupied islands. We sometimes had to cross sections of open sea in order to get to a neighboring island.

On the ocean we rode in motor launches or large sail boats. Those boats are very narrow, about four or five feet wide. Many of them were dug out of tree trunks with masts about fifteen feet high. They did not have keels, so when the wind blew, the sail would tip them over if they didn't have outriggers. Outriggers were made by fastening two poles across the boat, one toward the bow of the boat and the other toward the stern. Then, to provide buoyancy they would tie several bamboos on each end of those poles, so that the bamboos were parallel with the hull of the boat about ten feet out on each side.

If the wind was very strong two or three sailors would get way out on the poles near the outriggers to balance it, holding on to ropes to keep from falling overboard. The severity of a storm was measured by how many men it took to keep the boat balanced. There would be a one-man storm, or a two-man storm or a three-man storm.

Some of the large sailing boats were used for carrying cargo. This would often fill the boat and be piled up above the hull. So there was a bamboo runway along the side of the boat where the sailors and passengers could walk or sit. I often slept out on the bamboo runway outside the boat, because the boats would be loaded with copra. That drying coconut meat was very hot, was fermenting, and was full of copra bugs. It wasn't anything you would want to lie on. It would be very uncomfortable. So I fixed myself up on that narrow bamboo runway about a foot wide, out over the water. It wasn't too bad. I just had to remember not to turn over, and above all not to fall overboard. Once or twice when the weather was rough, I tied myself to that runway so I wouldn't fall overboard.

In that part of the world we had sudden severe storms that lasted maybe fifteen minutes, and then were gone. The water gets very rough and it rains.

One day we were returning home from the southern part of the island of Catanduanes when a severe storm arose, somewhat like those on the sea of Galilee. There were about two men on the outriggers of the boat. Needless to say, I was wide awake and holding on for dear life.

Another time we took off from northern Catanduanes in a motor launch when we struck very rough weather. Things on deck were falling all over. We had to hold on to keep our chairs from tipping over. I remember holding on to some statue, just barely keeping it from falling over. We were so seasick that we didn't much care what happened. As evening was falling, we got into the lee of an island, giving us calm and a good nights rest. There were no stores, and we had no food. But the next morning the crew netted some fish. Breakfast that morning was nothing but fish. It was delicious!

On another trip near the Caramoan peninsula, we were going around the point in a small motor boat to a place just east of Naga. No one knew what the weather was like at sea. It was very dark when we left the river and we hoped they knew where they were going. At first, there was enough light from the sky for us to see the coast dimly. When we got out to sea, we encountered extremely rough stormy weather. It got so bad the sailors decided to go back. By that time, it was so dark that I couldn't see a thing. Anxiously, I wondered whether they could find their way back into that river. How they ever found the mouth of the river, I don't know. There were no lights to guide them. Somehow, we got back to the place where we had started and I slept on a dining table that night. That was before I developed my hammock.

One time we drove to a place near Naga. We came to a large river that we had to cross by ferry. Ferries, in our part of the Philippines were essentially very small floating barges just large enough to carry one or two cars or a bus. Usually there would be a cable from one shore to the other and a pulley ran along the cable to keep the ferry on course from one side of the river to the other, as the ferry battled the river current. Men would pole the barge across the river or propel it by pulling on the cable.

After the ferry took us to the other side of the river, we drove to the house of friends where we left our car and hiked up to the place where our meetings were held.

While we were there, a typhoon came. When we drove back to the river, it had overflowed its banks. It was so flooded that they couldn't bring the ferry to its usual landing places on either side of the river. Both landings were in the midst of the flood. They brought the ferry as close to shore as they could, and we drove the car through muddy water about a foot and a half deep and up some planks onto the ferry. When we got to the other side several men, standing deep in the water, had to push that ferry along the road until it grounded close to the railroad track. And then, once again with planks from the ferry out into the murky water we were able to drive off the ferry, over the railroad, and onto the highway.

That was a hair-raising experience. Of course they had somebody standing by the planks to guide us. But, from where I was sitting in the car it wasn't easy to see those planks. It was frightening to drive onto planks that you couldn't see under muddy water.

Our work of preaching and teaching was challenging and fulfilling. The people were responsive to the Gospel. Believers were being baptized and were uniting with the church. The church was growing and strong Filipino leadership was emerging.

In 1939, after nearly twenty years of challenging service, we left Legaspi for our regular furlough in the States, assuming we would return the following year. But our plans are often not God's plans. Instead, we were assigned to Manila, where my second career as an administrator began.

Arthur, Anthony, *Deliverance at Los Baños*, St. Martin's Press, New York, 1985.

Terrill Baker, Richard, *Darkness of the Sun, The Story of Christianity in the Japanese Empire*, Abingdon Cokesbury Press, New York, Nashville 1947.

Connaughton, Richard, and others, *The Battle for Manila*, Bloomsbury, London, 1997.

Flanagan, Jr., Lt. Gen. E.M. *The Los Baños Raid*, A Jove Book, New York, 1987.

History Channel TV Program, *Rescue at Dawn The Los Baños Raid* Cat No AAE 71342.

Ringler, John M., *The Los Baños Raid*, On the Internet

Santos, Terry, *The Provisional Recon. Platoon – Spearhead of the Los Baños Raid*, On the Internet.

Wheeler, Robert A., *The Angels Came at Dawn*, On the Internet.

Wikipedia, The Free Encyclopedia, *Raid at Los Baños*, On the Internet.

About the Author

Donald P. Smith grew up in the Philippines, until he was seventeen years old. With his wife Verna, he lived in Manila for five years just after World War II. He wrote this factual account from the war as though it was an autobiography by Stephen L Smith, making extensive use of recorded conversations with his father, and with his younger brother Paul.

Stephen and Viola Smith celebrated their 60th Wedding Anniversary in 1977 in Watsonville, California, where Stephen completed his "Third Career" as Associate Pastor of the Watsonville Presbyterian Church.

CPSIA information can be obtained at www.ICGtesting.com
Printed in the USA
BVOW021353040312

284317BV00003B/35/A

9 781434 329677